ACCOUNT-BASED MARKETING

ACCOUNT-BASED MARKETING

How to Target and Engage the Companies That Will Grow Your Revenue

Chris
Golec

Peter
Isaacson

Jessica
Fewless

Contents

ACCOUNT-BASED MARKETING

1 | The Sweet Spot

Why Now Is a Better Time to Try ABM Instead of Five Years Ago or Five Years from Now

Crystal balls are silly, right? We all know that it's impossible to predict the future. Take the stock market for example: if someone could predict its movements, that person could retire in a day and be a billionaire in a month. It's also impossible to predict other short-term events like who will win the Super Bowl, or be next year's pop music sensation.

Even so, accurate crystal balls do exist—if you know how to look at the right things. For example, demographics are highly predictable: we can confidently forecast the median age of a country's population even 10 or 20 years from now.

Another clear trend: one by one, industries are being transformed by technology. Some industries benefit sooner than others. Technology has allowed the 140-year-old telephone to become infinitely more useful as a smartphone. Farming has gone from the iron plow to GPS-mapped fields that get precise amounts of fertilizers every few feet in order to maximize crop yields.

This book is about another trend we can confidently predict: it's the turn of business-to-business (B2B) marketing and sales to benefit from the technology revolution. We are at the early stages of an astonishing transformation in B2B marketing, made possible by data science, and aided by cheaper computing power and storage, as we'll discuss later. Companies that recognize these elements coming together will be positioned to lead their industries in reputation, relationships, and revenue. Their competitors who are late to the party will wonder what happened.

Just as recognizing trends too late can mean that all you get are the crumbs, it's also possible to adopt technology too early: the first attempts at applying technology can be buggy, time consuming, and frustrating. It can be enough to put you off the whole idea unless you're willing at first to take one step back for every two steps forward.

This book is also about how right now, we're at the sweet spot where mature technology meets B2B marketing: we're far enough along that the technology has been tested, refined, and proven. Yet we're early enough in the revolution that most industries have not yet been dominated by companies that recognize the sweet spot, act on it, and have become the leaders. That's the opportunity before you right now.

To be more specific, the opportunity relates to Account-Based Marketing, or ABM. In the pages to come we'll become intimately familiar with the workings of ABM, but for now let's use this definition:

> Account-Based Marketing enables marketers to identify and target the accounts they value most. Accounts can be segmented in many ways, like prospect or customer. That's not new. What's new is this: among other capabilities, ABM allows you to personalize the marketing experience to your target accounts *before they ever identify themselves to you*. And you can scale it to 30, 300, or 3,000 accounts to support your business objectives.

"In your dreams," you say? "Pie in the sky," you say? No. ABM is a tested and proven approach that gives you insights into what your prospects are thinking and doing. In a sales environment in which business is won or lost on slim margins, ABM enables you to enjoy a substantial advantage over your competitors who are likely doing business the way their parents and grandparents did it.

Is This Book for You?

At this point, you may be asking yourself a reasonable question: "Chris, Peter, and Jessica wrote this book, they work at Demandbase, and they offer ABM-related solutions. Is this book going to be one long sales pitch for their stuff?"

Relax. There are a lot of great ABM technologies out there today, with more on the way. That's what makes ABM such a vibrant category. But this book does not focus on any single vendor or any single technology. We intend to answer the following questions:

- What exactly is ABM, and how is it different from the way marketing was done in the past?
- What companies are right for ABM and what ones are not? (Because nothing is right for everyone.)
- How can I determine if ABM will work in my company? (It needs to be done in such a way that you don't spend a ton of time and money before you know the answer.)
- What are best practices and also pitfalls to avoid so as to maximize the contribution of ABM to our bottom line?

Our guess is that you've been around the block a few times when it comes to witnessing fads that come and go in business. You have a healthy skepticism about something you're told has the potential to make a big difference in your revenues. It's not that you're cynical that nothing will work—you just need proof and details before taking the next step.

Our further guess is that you're in the marketing department of a B2B business, given that the book title is about account-based marketing, and not selling directly to consumers. If you happen to be in sales, you will also get a great deal from this book: you'll love how we advocate a different approach for marketing, getting away from delivering volumes of leads that you have no interest in pursuing, to working with you to generate interest from the accounts you actually care about.

If we're even partly right about your situation, then you're in for a treat: we will show you a smarter way to attract and persuade the customers you most want to close and win.

Now let's look at why ABM is such a fundamental improvement on the inefficiencies that make up much of traditional marketing.

Fujitsu on ABM:

"We've proven that ABM is a successful part of what we do in marketing. Without ABM we'd be struggling to achieve our KPIs. So ABM is kind of a hero."

—*Head of Account-Based and Deal-Based Marketing, EMEIA Fujitsu*

What Would a World-Class Marketing Strategy Include?

In his book, *The 7 Habits of Highly Effective People*, Stephen Covey calls one of those habits "Begin with the end in mind."[1] Let's consider that approach and try to answer the following question:"If we were designing a zero-waste, world-class marketing system, what would it look like?" Here's our take on how we would define the characteristics of such a system—and the degree to which ABM meets those characteristics:

1. **You don't waste efforts on people who are not available or qualified to buy what you have to offer.** Some leads may be qualified but currently locked into multiyear contracts. Then again, someone may be typing in the keywords you're targeting and paying for in your pay-per-click campaign, and this person is merely writing a research paper in college. Either way, you would save time and money if you could filter out such leads.

---

[1] Stephen R. Covey, *The 7 Habits of Highly Effective People: Powerful Lessons in Personal Change* (New York: Simon & Schuster, 2014).

ABM allows you to do just that. Sure, anybody can come to your website or stroll up to your booth at an event. Some of those visitors may even end up buying from you. But in terms of your outbound efforts, ABM focuses your resources on your target accounts.

2. **Down the road after you implement both ABM strategy and technology, you will be able to detect the earliest stages when qualified and available prospects are not just surfing, but are in the market for a solution.** Imagine how great it would be to engage with prospects at just the right time in the buying journey: they're not merely casually browsing, but seem to be on the hunt for solutions. At the same time, you want to be able to know when they're not so far along that their minds are made up.

   As you'll see later in this book, technology deployed to support an ABM strategy gives you the ability to gauge where your target accounts are in their buying journey, and what it is that they're focused on buying. This allows you not to waste messages that are mismatched with the mindset of those target accounts.

3. **You will be able to deliver a personalized message to target accounts, even before they ever fill out a form on your site and give you any personal details.** For years the best you could hope for on your site was to get people to fill out your form in exchange for a white paper, webinar, or other piece of content. That can work okay except for the people who've been burned by filling out a form, because they were hounded afterward. They will not complete the form, or they'll use bogus details and a throwaway email address.

   With ABM, you can not only serve up a page that's customized to target accounts when they visit your site, but you have the luxury of deciding the extent of that personalization. Highly relevant messages served with pinpoint accuracy enable you to avoid a lot of generalized, semi-effective messaging.

4. **Marketing and Sales are in sync so that Marketing delivers the kind of leads that Sales wants.** Have you ever

delivered leads to Sales, only to find out that they didn't follow through on them? Yeah, we know the feeling. What if we told you that a world does exist in which the kind of leads you deliver are just the kind that Sales wants?

When an ABM strategy is working properly, that's precisely what happens. We said, "Working properly" because sometimes people think they're following ABM when in fact they're misapplying it or only partly applying it. We'll get into this in much more detail later. We'll also give you many real-world cases of ABM facilitating Marketing and Sales to work together and not at cross-purposes.

5. **Marketing's budget is calibrated so that as leads get closer to becoming revenue, more dollars are spent on them.** It's always been the case that a few choice prospects would merit the expense of VIP or exec experiences. However, it's also been the case that enormous amounts of budget gets spent on spray-and-pray activities, in the hope that the more that leads of any kind get loaded into the hopper up top, the more will trickle down to closed-won status. Talk about waste.

With ABM it's possible to synchronize expenses so that as target accounts progress through the pipeline, they get progressively more attention and resources. It's certainly how they want to be treated, and it's possible to do so without increasing your budget. In fact, we'll explain how your expenses might even drop while simultaneously enhancing the experience of those on your target account list.

Pushback

You and we are in the marketing profession, and we know that some of the best customers are the ones who start off with lots of questions. They want to believe what you're telling them, but they first need to square it with their understanding of how things actually work.

At this early stage in the book, we expect that you have plenty of questions about ABM and how it may or may not apply to your situation. Throughout the book we'll address the likely questions that relate to whichever aspect we're discussing at the moment. For now, let's address a few things that might be on your mind from the get-go:

"What's actually new here? Target marketing has been around for ages." This is where labels can sometimes get in the way. Computers have been around for many decades, but early computers only have a vague resemblance to current ones.

The general concept of ABM has been around for about 20 years. Initially it went by the names of Strategic Account Marketing or Target Account Marketing to match the Target Account Selling approach used by many sales teams.

For many years, and in fact decades, it was common for organizations to focus on a relatively small number of named accounts. Marketing initiatives like customer dinners, executive briefings, or even one-off webinars were high-touch and personalized. They took a lot of time and individual attention to be effective, and were therefore not very scalable. Most companies could afford this level of attention for a handful of accounts, and the biggest companies might have had the resources to extend this high-touch approach to at most a very few dozen accounts.

By around the year 2000, we started to see two major improvements, in the form of marketing automation systems (MAS) and customer relationship management (CRM) systems. At last, digital marketing systems had gone beyond spreadsheets and word processing tools, and began to be useful for large marketing organizations.

The limitation was that these systems were focused on email, which is a fine communication channel but very quickly became loaded with spam. This was the golden age of spam, when everyone had an email address, but companies like Google were years away from developing effective spam filters. As a reaction to all this spam, response rates dropped.

These systems had two other limitations: they focused only on individuals, and they were reactive. They required the capture of contact information at an event or through a web form before you could market to that individual.

ABM grew out of the realization by a few marketers that the account was the missing link between Marketing and Sales. If those teams could align around accounts and revenue, then they both would be pulling in the same direction.

> Chris (Demandbase founder) has been in B2B sales and marketing his whole career, starting at DuPont and then at GE. He held a number of marketing and technical sales roles. For example, for one job, he managed 25 accounts in a region. The job was not to get new customers in, as much as to maintain this base of customers—who brought in $25 million annually—by owning those relationships. For years, he did account-based marketing and account-based selling, but it was all analog.
>
> Chris then co-founded a company to help large businesses identify and manage their worldwide supplier base. They sold into companies like Apple, GE, and Dell. He was running marketing and was surprised at the lack of tools and functionality.
>
> The company got acquired and Chris then got into consulting, helping small businesses study their revenue plan and reverse-engineer what had to happen in marketing to hit that revenue plan. He would be asked by VCs to analyze their portfolio companies and often had to report: "Your companies are missing their revenue goals even before the sales team starts selling. That's because they're getting all these leads from companies that will never buy."
>
> Over these various jobs, Chris realized that the suitable account is the missing link between sales and marketing. Take pay-per-click ads, for example. If you have 100 leads, maybe only four will be worth anything because the rest are the wrong industry, wrong size, or wrong person coming to the site.
>
> Marketing tools traditionally focused on B2C: the tools were about age, gender, and income. In B2B, it's about industry and revenue instead. Chris set out to change that tool situation when he started Demandbase. The focus became how to use technology to enable ABM to be scalable.
>
> Chris likes to say: "All marketing is better when you know whom you're talking to."

Technology eventually reached a point at which it could support and expand the ABM focus on high-value accounts. To put things in perspective, in 1967 it cost around one million dollars to store one megabyte of data.[2] These days, some companies will give you a million times more data storage—one terabyte—just for free, for using their cloud applications.[3]

Technology has enabled the originally manual process of ABM to be scaled and optimized. In addition to inexpensive storage, ABM is further enhanced by massive computing power, the relatively new field of data science, and more sophisticated website-personalization tools. It has only been when these technologies matured and were combined that ABM at scale became possible. Figure 1.1 shows a summary of how ABM has evolved.

"So what then are these new capabilities that were previously impossible?" First, they enable you to get beyond individuals and look at entire accounts, which is what's needed in the B2B world. As consumers, we usually make decisions on our own or perhaps after consulting one or two others. In the B2B world, the average decision-making group includes more than six buyers.[4] ABM allows you to get a good idea of how many people from a given target account are researching a topic.

Second, ABM allows you to discover and identify accounts that are showing buying signals and real intent in your products and services—before they ever raise their hand and provide contact information on your site.

Third, ABM provides your sales team with insights and information they need on the target accounts and decision makers, so they can close deals faster. Harvey Mackay is a bestselling author and founder of Mackay Envelope. He developed what was known as the Mackay 66: it was 66 different pieces of information on key decision makers in B2B accounts. He required that no salesperson could return from

---

[2] https://www.computerworld.com/article/3182207/data-storage/cw50-data-storage-goes-from-1m-to-2-cents-per-gigabyte.html
[3] https://www.computerworld.com/article/2490087/cloud-computing/microsoft-boosts-onedrive-storage-to-free-terabyte.html
[4] https://hbr.org/2017/03/the-new-sales-imperative

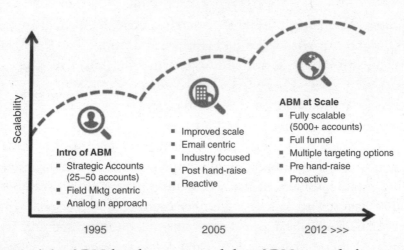

Figure 1.1   ABM has been around, but ABM at scale is a more recent development

the field without collecting at least one new piece of information.[5] That was many years ago. Now some ABM systems collect as many as 200 *billion* data points per month on accounts and people. They provide the background and context that your salespeople can use to maximize rapport, engagement, and sales.

Fourth, ABM allows you to deliver a personalized, relevant experience on your website to visitors from these accounts. After all, if you sell direct-current motors and turbine engines and you know that Acme Industries uses devices that could incorporate only your turbines, it makes no sense to show your direct-current motors to visitors from Acme. What's cool is you can deliver these tailored experiences in real time.

The fifth capability is huge: ABM allows you to do all of this **at scale.** You can target hundreds or even thousands of qualified accounts, and each one can be the recipient of carefully tailored information that matches where the account is in the buyer's journey.

Important note: ABM is not an app or service the way a CRM tool is. ABM uses technology, but it is ultimately a strategy. That's why you cannot just buy yourself "an ABM" and plug it in at your

---

[5] http://www.harveymackay.com/wp-content/uploads/2016/01/mackay66.pdf

company. You need to build the strategy, align groups within your company, set up certain communications and reporting systems, and then integrate the technology into it. There will be much more on this later.

"Given the level of personalization you describe, ABM must cost a fortune to implement." As we discuss in detail in the next chapter, ABM requires that you and Sales co-create a target account list. Because these are the accounts that are the most qualified and most able to deliver the revenue you seek, your efforts become focused on a smaller number of accounts compared to the old way of doing business. As a result, it's often possible to keep overall marketing expenses at or even below pre-ABM levels.

As we'll also discuss later, ABM can play a major role in keeping your customers happy over the long term. This can result in reduced churn, lower ongoing expenses, and longer lifetime values.

"We are interested in improving our B2B effectiveness, but how do I know that this methodology will work in our business? You don't. (We told you this was going to be a no-BS book.)

ABM is not suitable for every company on the planet, just as no solution works for everyone. That's why we will spend a lot of time in the coming pages to explain how you can run a small pilot program in your company—before you ever buy any technology from us or anyone else—so you can see if ABM works in your situation.

At the end of the day, that's the only valid response to this valid question, right? Because if someone tells you, "Yeah, we don't know your exact business but this is perfect for your business" you know that's nonsense.

Key Gains of an ABM Strategy

We talked earlier about how until recently, technology had not advanced to the point that would allow companies to use an ABM strategy at scale. We also talked about how ABM is not merely a tool, but instead a strategy that uses technology, alignment of goals and compensation, and a high degree of communication, among other practices, in order to work at maximum effectiveness.

What can an organization look forward to once it has these elements in place and working? You can expect some remarkable things.

First, you'll see an end to the conflicts and disconnects that have historically existed between Marketing and Sales. That conflict has traditionally been rooted in a disconnect between the focus of those units. Marketing typically focused on individuals and Sales usually focused on accounts. Sure, there may have been exceptions and times when Marketing and Sales were in sync, but for the most part, these different areas of focus led to frustration for both groups.

ABM has the potential—and a proven record in many companies—to also shift Marketing's focus to accounts, much to the relief of Sales. And it doesn't stop there: as we'll see in a later chapter, the focus becomes centered on specific target accounts. This way everyone's energies and resources are focused on the same targets, and that results in closing deals more quickly.

Second—and this is a big one—your organization will ultimately be able to focus on the quality of leads and not merely on the quantity. This is where the "strategy" part comes in, because this mindset shift will be a challenge for some at first. Traditionally, companies have for the most part focused on quantity—pouring leads into the top of the funnel in the hope that a few would eventually work their way down to closed–won business.

Think about how painful this process has been for all parties: Marketing needed to work triple time to fill up that funnel because close rates have historically been a fraction of a percent. Sales then had to attempt somehow to sift and sort all of those leads, knowing full well that most would never amount to anything. Both parties needed to play the quantity game because it felt like it was the only game in town. From all the B2B companies we talk to, we find that anywhere between 50 to 75 percent of leads—depending on program type and corporate culture—never get followed up. We suspect that this may not come as a total surprise to you.

The game-changer is ABM. When you have key performance indicators (KPIs) and compensation in line with lead quality—we'll show you how to do this later—then Marketing can focus on bringing in high-quality leads that are more likely to buy from you. That, in turn, allows Sales to focus more on those very same leads from the accounts they care about. They have more time to focus on them now that they're not chasing as many dead ends.

The third benefit is that your organization will increase efficiency and move closer to that zero-waste strategy we talked about earlier. Once you have your target account list agreed upon, you can focus your resources where they will do the most good. For example, instead of generating five lower-quality leads at five different companies, you will be able to generate, say, three leads from the decision makers in one of your target companies. Now you'll be in a position to influence the buying decision more effectively in that company.

Once you have a defined set of target accounts, coupled with the ABM platform, your programs can become focused on proactively delivering your message to those accounts instead of hoping that they come to your site and fill out a form. You'll be able to use sophisticated buyer-intent methods to engage them with the appropriate message for the stage they're in, and move them along the buyer's journey.

Marketing and Sales will be doing all of this with more company intelligence than you've had before, again thanks to the ABM platform. You'll know more about these accounts in your own meetings and when going into meetings with those accounts. This added intelligence will enable Sales to prioritize these leads even more effectively so as to maximize the chances of converting the leads into opportunities and eventually into revenue.

How to Make a Smooth Transition into ABM

It can be scary and downright unproductive when it's necessary to make a complete break with how things have been done in the past, whether it's a new corporate software system or other major change. Fortunately, no such chasm needs to be crossed when you move along on your ABM journey.

When we work with companies around the world, we explain that it's possible to ease your way into an ABM strategy by taking it in three phases.

Phase 1: New lens. This is where you look at your existing world, but in the new context of accounts and revenue as opposed to leads and volume. Your goal is to evaluate and you do that by developing metrics and reporting that accurately describes your current state, before ABM. Having that baseline is crucial, so when you begin to get data from your pilot program—also something that happens in this phase—it's not in a vacuum but in relation to your baseline. The pilot also gives you a chance to figure out what works and what doesn't based on your organization's needs.

Phase 2: New programs. In this phase, you already have the data and experience that came from running the pilot. Now it's time to clone and expand that experience so that ABM becomes the marketing and sales strategy for the whole organization. You still are trying different approaches because your company is not quite like any other. In this phase, your goal is to optimize: you home in on the best practices and processes for your company, optimize your budget, and also evaluate your tech stack in light of ABM.

Phase 3: New thinking. Only in this third phase is the objective to go all in. It's after you've had a chance to see ABM close up and see its results on your bottom line and on organizational harmony. At this stage, you continue to refine your team and practices so you can execute like the high-performance machine that you've become. You operate at all three levels—one-to-one, one-to-few, and one-to-many —and your regret is that you didn't know about ABM sooner.

~ ~ ~

Now that you have the big picture of what this book will cover, let's get into the key building blocks that can form the basis of ABM in your company.

2

Building Blocks

Foundational Concepts in ABM

Let's assume that the concept of ABM sounds intriguing to you, and you want to understand more about what it involves and how it might fit into your organization.

In Chapter 1, we touched upon a few of the technology-based benefits of an ABM strategy. Let's now look more deeply into the organizational benefits that some of the largest companies on the planet—and many smaller ones too—are finding as they apply ABM to their B2B goals.

Organizational Benefits of ABM

There's been an explosion in recent years in the number of tools relating to ABM. Some of those tools are what is known as "point solutions" because they attempt to deliver one single benefit. Although there may be a place for such tools, our experience is that companies get the very most out of ABM when a strategy—not a tool—is at the heart of the effort. It's otherwise not uncommon for someone to say, "We tried that ABM thing once. It didn't do much for us. ABM doesn't work."

We will discuss later the specific steps you can take to create an effective strategy. When you in fact have a strong foundation for ABM, you can look forward to four benefits:

1. **You at last can focus on the best opportunities at scale.** As we said earlier, companies have always been able to focus on a relative handful of named accounts, but not more than that. Historically, if you didn't have detailed information on accounts beyond that handful, then you were destined to play the numbers game. That hopper better stay full, given how few leads ever turn into revenue.

    ABM gives your organization the confidence to convert from a quantity game to a quality one. Chasing fewer leads means more resources can be devoted to the best opportunities, thus leading to higher pipeline velocity and higher closed–won rates.

2. **Marketing and Sales become aligned.** ABM requires a shift in Marketing's focus away from individuals and toward accounts, which is exactly how Sales looks at the world. The historical tensions that exist between the two units don't all magically disappear, but they are substantially reduced. There is further good news: as your organization starts to reap the benefits of your ABM strategy, the Sales team will lean in more and more to collaborate with you and contribute to your success.

3. **Customers receive a better experience.** Focusing on a limited number of target accounts means that you can deliver a much more personalized experience to those accounts. Instead of focusing solely on demand generation, Marketing will work hand in hand with Sales throughout the buyer's journey to mirror their message to the entire stakeholder committee that's researching your products online. This type of consistency will help speed up the sales process.

4. **Marketing becomes connected to revenue.** A fundamental, universal need for business has always been to generate revenue

because you can't take leads to the bank. ABM resolves the disconnect through which Marketing could be rewarded for generating leads that did not ultimately generate revenue. By linking Marketing's goals not only to accounts but to accounts that produce revenue, at last the organizational gears can mesh properly and work in the same direction.

One Size Never Fits All

There are as many flavors of ABM as there are companies using it, but even so, it's possible to group the variations into three levels, as seen in Figure 2.1.

One-to-One ABM

We've discussed the one-to-one form of ABM, which has been practiced basically forever. When Peter was head of worldwide field marketing at Adobe, it was called "Target Account Marketing." They

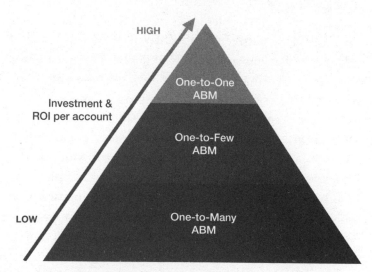

Figure 2.1   The Three Main Types of ABM
Source: **ITSMA and ABM Leadership Alliance Account-Based Marketing Benchmarking Survey, July 2017.**

worked with Sales and selected around 20 accounts. Then they pains-takingly and laboriously created what were known as "account plans" that were five to 10 pages long. The effort was worth it because Sales absolutely loved the detail Marketing provided, including org charts, who the decision makers were, key selling propositions, and so forth.

The bad news was that even though Adobe was a large organiza-tion with substantial resources, it practically killed them to prepare these reports on just 20 accounts.

Consider where we are today when ABM is applied to one-to-one marketing: we can provide org charts and lists of decision makers. The key selling propositions are now even better because we can use data science to discern not only where these key accounts have been searching but what they've searched for. We can also now discern important elements of their intent, based on what they're looking for. We will have more on this in a moment.

With one-to-one ABM, the focus tends to be on existing key accounts, even though it's possible to do this level of personalization on a target account that is not yet a customer.

One-to-Few ABM

This is a hybrid level of personalization in which we're dealing with clusters of accounts that share similar characteristics. These clusters typically contain five to 15 accounts, based on these common char-acteristics or issues.

For example, a supplier of oil well equipment might create a cluster of accounts around "fracking wastewater management" that has to do with how to handle the environmental issues surrounding oil well fracking. Another cluster might be around "drill string cou-plings." Both clusters have the common denominator of oil well equipment, but the separate clusters describe challenges in which people searching for those problems have highly specific needs.

By creating a "one-to-few" grouping, you can still get highly spe-cific about the desired goal of your target market, but it's at a slightly more general level that several companies may share. It's not so spe-cific as to be relevant to only one company.

Why would you ever choose to do one-to-few ABM instead of one-to-one? Because you can effectively speak to those common characteristics and a more-personalized treatment may not be necessary.

One-to-few ABM usually focuses on existing key accounts with these similar issues, as well as new accounts that match the same profile.

One-to-Many ABM

This form of targeting is most often used for generating a higher volume of opportunities from your target account list. If, for example, you have five accounts in your one-to-one program, and another 45 in your one-to-few, you might have 1000-plus in your one-to-many tier. It still includes personalization, to the extent that certain characteristics are common to hundreds of accounts: maybe industry, stage in the sales cycle, a particular focused product, geography, and so forth.

As Figure 2.1 indicates, as you move up the pyramid to the more personalized, high-touch form of ABM, not only do you invest more time and resources into those accounts, you also expect higher returns from those investments. It all gets back to carefully selecting the target account list—which we discuss in detail in Chapter 4.

Of course, there is no sharp line separating these forms of ABM. Companies don't adopt one single approach. Instead, a company may have one-to-one ABM in place for the most critical accounts and be doing, for example, one-to-many marketing for the launch of a product into a relatively new market.

It comes down to an optimization decision. You have a certain budget and headcount that must cover existing accounts and new ones, and you also have business objectives. We've found that the best way to optimize is through scenarios.

"What if we take this group of accounts and apply one-to-one to them? That will leave us with this amount of budget to do one-to-few with our other accounts. But that will get us to only 50 percent of our Revenue Target for the year. So maybe we take a little budget from one-to-one and one-to-few so that we can address an additional 1,000 accounts through our one-to-many approach." You're doing this planning in conjunction with Sales, of course. It may be that Sales has a different take on which accounts should get what level of attention. But when you come out the other end, both sides should feel like they have contributed to the strategy, and thus will be committed to its success.

It's not too different from the push-and-pull that you're accustomed to when doing budgeting and planning. Your first draft is unlikely to be the best, because it's only through a detailed discussion that you collectively become aware of all the factors at play and the best compromise that will balance them.

Of course, these decisions are not set in stone, and as you get new information, they can be adjusted. In fact, accounts may shift between tiers based on this information. For example, if it becomes clear that an account in your one-to-one program has nowhere for your company to grow its revenue, it might be time to move it into one-to-few. You still want to give the account some extra attention to retain it because it is probably among your top revenue generating accounts, but it might not make sense to spend at the one-to-one level to do so. In taking this action, you free up the resources to move a new account into one-to-one with a large potential for growth.

Just be sure not to adjust them too often, because that can quickly become a form of rudderless indecision. As a very general rule, we suggest that you lock in your decisions and directions, if possible, for at least a calendar quarter or longer, depending on your sales cycle. That way you're giving the campaigns time to get implemented and produce some meaningful data on which to base more refined decisions.

Data Is at the Core of an ABM Strategy

Of course, every B2B company is already awash in data, but data is used differently in a company that follows an ABM strategy. First, you will use data intensively to create your target account list. As we discuss in Chapter 4, you'll base your decisions on data that goes well beyond wanting to focus merely on top accounts, or on Fortune 500 companies.

Second, data informs your website strategy. Instead of just having a relatively static page for every product and service, an ABM-focused company will combine static pages with dynamically created content and serve it up based on the individual visitors to your site.

Finally, in the ABM world, data informs your choice of marketing programs. For example, you won't produce webinars because that's what everyone in your industry does. You'll produce them because you have hard data to show that your target account list is especially responsive to that form of communication.

Detecting Intent

Data will also allow you to detect intent. For example, imagine that you can see the search terms of someone named Ellen, who is interested in oil well fracking. If she types in "fracking," that's pretty vague. Based on that search term, it's highly likely that she is not in the oil and gas industry. Maybe she's doing a term paper on the evolution of fracking. Maybe she's a buyer of equipment at a very early stage—we can't tell yet.

Then you see that Ellen typed in "fracking suppliers." Now she's narrowed her searches down to specific suppliers and not just a general term. Hmmm, still pretty vague, but more specific than before. Ellen then searches for "Halliburton versus Schlumberger Production Optimization." Now it's clear that she is not writing a term paper, but is comparing oil field suppliers. Her decision about which one to go with is very much in play. (It's a great time to be showing her ads about "How to compare production optimization solutions.") By the time Ellen types in "ResFlood Multizonal Selective Injection System alternatives" we have an extremely strong idea of her intentions: this person knows the specific solutions she's after and now the only likely question is who meets her current needs on price, availability, and so on.

That's a simple example, and data scientists get much more sophisticated at discerning intent from the literally billions of data points they crunch. Also keep in mind that Ellen is likely to be only one of several decision makers at her company. The power of ABM is its ability to detect intent for Ellen, but also for other people at her company who are coming at the challenge from different perspectives and levels of knowledge.

The beautiful thing about discerning intent is that once the artificial intelligence (AI) and machine learning has been created, tested, and refined around the question of intent, you can receive reports about the likely intent of your target account list, even if that list numbers in the thousands. You may still choose to group accounts into the one-to-one, one-to-few, or one-to-many segments for purposes of delivering your messages, but the messaging can be more refined and effective now that you are armed with details surrounding intent.

The Six Areas of Focus for ABM

To continue our discussion about the major components of an ABM strategy, let's look at six areas of focus when you're applying ABM across your sales funnel, as seen in Figure 2.2.

Figure 2.2 Six Areas of Focus for ABM Across Your Sales Funnel

1. Identify

All companies focus on certain accounts that they deem to be important. The problem occurs when that list is cobbled together haphazardly over time or by using seat-of-the-pants logic along the lines of: "It goes without saying that we should include *these* accounts...."

Your ABM strategy will be dead in the water without taking the time to build a solid foundation by focusing on the right set of accounts, with decisions driven by data, and in tight collaboration with your sales team. It will be worth the time and attention you give to this phase to make sure you get it right from the get-go. We cover this critical element in great detail in Chapter 4.

Mini-Case Study

A company that's the leader in its industry came to us for ABM consulting. When we asked what their goal was for ABM, they said, "We've recently decided to eliminate many of our smaller, mid-market accounts by raising our subscription fees significantly, and focusing on enterprise accounts. We've created an initial target account list of them."

"Okay," we said, "what are your goals for implementing ABM in your organization?"

"We want to raise awareness among our enterprise prospects."

The initial hypothesis, therefore, was that enterprise companies just didn't know enough about this organization. Fair enough. But before we took any action, we wanted to confirm that hypothesis. We ran an analysis of the actual visitors to this company's site, and segmented the results by their target account list and non-target accounts.

Check this out: it wasn't an awareness issue at all. We were able to confirm that many of the target companies already knew about this organization and were coming to their site—but that

(continued)

Mini-Case Study *(cont'd)*

the target accounts were bouncing at nearly twice the rate of mid-market companies! We now had a new hypothesis: the site did not reflect the identity and needs of enterprise customers.

The company then created a variation of the home page to show to its target account list of enterprise customers, emphasizing that segment of the market. For example, it showcased enterprise-level logos and simply used the word "enterprise" more, while staying appropriate about it. When the results were tallied, bounce rates for the target account list went down by 50 percent.

This brings up another example of the power of ABM: even before you implement the entire system, you can gain insights into what's going on—and not going on—with your existing marketing and sales efforts. Performing a company-level analysis of the current visitors to your website is one of the more no-brainer actions to take early on.

2. Attract

Now that you've identified your target account list (again, more on this in Chapter 4), the next main area to focus on relates to attraction. To be more specific, you don't simply want to "attract more of our target audience" because that's so vague as to be immeasurable.

Try to determine what success looks like with respect to attraction. First, it must be directly tied to your target account list. No longer should you be looking at pure volume metrics for campaigns like downloads, RSVPs, booth scans, and so forth. Our focus now is on quality over quantity. Therefore, take a look at the quantity and the percent of downloads from your target accounts. This will tell you things like: Are you increasing your effectiveness at reaching your target accounts? Are your programs resonating with those accounts? If your numbers are going up, but the percentage coming from your target accounts is going down, then you have to ask yourself whether that program was really a success.

Another important measure of attraction is the number of unique individuals you are engaging at a target account, also known as account penetration. Because most B2B sales involve multiple decision makers, this measurement can become a type of leading indicator of the interest shown by the target account in your offerings. Your goal is to deliver relevant messages to everyone who will weigh in on the purchase decision. The more individuals you can engage, the more air cover you're providing to the sales team to help reinforce their conversations with the buyer. How this might come to life is with a goal for your field marketing team to get two or more attendees to an event from each account you invite.

When it comes to the methods you can use to attract the accounts, there's no shortage. Here are just a few:

- Sponsored events
- Field marketing
- Webinars
- Advertising
- Email marketing
- Content syndication
- Direct mail
- Search engine marketing
- Social media
- PR

How then should you optimize your marketing mix? The best way is to look at each of these methods and ask yourself five questions.

Question 1: Can I target my account list?

For example, if you're evaluating the events coming up in the next few months, start with your target account list and compare it to the companies that will be attending those events. Our own internal threshold at Demandbase is that we need to see at least 30 percent of the attendees at a show are on our target account list, or we're likely not to sponsor the show.

We will disregard this guideline in rare situations, like Dreamforce, for example, simply because of the sheer size of the show. In that example, we know that a vast majority of our target account list will be in attendance, so we build programs accordingly to make sure we can separate them from the masses and engage with them directly throughout the show. In either case, it's not about how many booth scans we can get but rather about building a presence that engages our target accounts through VIP dinners, roundtable breakfasts, a private meeting suite, and so forth.

For those events that don't meet that threshold, however, we don't necessarily completely walk away. If we see that a dozen target accounts will be at a show, we might pay for someone from Sales to attend the event, work with their sales development rep (SDR) to set up meetings with those specific accounts, and invite them to a really nice dinner, or other type of higher-touch experience. Those accounts will be the recipients of more attention than we would have provided under the old model, and our time and budget are concentrated on the accounts we really care about.

Question 2: Can I provide a relevant message?

Your message no longer needs to be "one size fits all." Advertising can now be personalized. Your website can now be personalized. Even direct mail can be personalized. So don't settle for a message that should resonate with most people. Find channels, vendors, and technology that allow you to get a relevant message, the message you specifically want, into the hands of your target accounts.

Question 3: Can I reach multiple stakeholders?

As we mentioned earlier, here's where B2C and B2B differ, big time. When competition is fierce, we need to influence as many decision makers in a target account as possible. In that case, social media may or may not be a good use of budget dollars. It will depend on your situation. Social media will be much more effective if the target industry is in the entertainment business than in the mining business. This also gets to the fact that our campaigns need to be multichannel. While one person might see your post on Twitter, a cube mate might not even have a Twitter account. But that same person will respond to an email, direct mail, or advertisement.

Question 4: Will it fit into my budget?

In Question 1 of this set, we gave an example in which typically costly initiatives like events can be pared down or reconfigured to focus on target accounts. Because ABM allows you to focus on fewer accounts with higher potential value, it's worth reviewing your spend with all marketing methods to see which ones can be adjusted based on this new mindset. Certain methods like content syndication or social media allow you to more easily tune the effort to the available budget.

Question 5: Can I provide more quality leads?

When you review the methods you used in the last period, which ones had the highest ROI? Remember, it's not about which ones provided the most leads, or even marketing qualified leads (MQLs) or sales accepted leads (SALs) (or name your top of funnel metric). It's about your ability to affect revenue. So which programs and program types produced the most leads that converted to pipeline that converted to closed–won business. Those are the programs in which you should invest more resources because they are a more direct line to revenue.

Question 6: Is this method as effective as others?

Here's where you rank–order the methods as best you can, based on your experience. Of course, it's important to use data whenever possible, and avoid conventional wisdom along the lines of "direct mail doesn't work anymore." You may find that the higher level of focus that comes from having a target account list enables you to make some methods work when they previously would not. For example, you may be able to use a highly targeted direct-mail campaign that uses FedEx to get past gatekeepers when that would have been prohibitively expensive in the old, non-targeted world.

Here's an example of what you might conclude after reviewing the marketing mix in light of these questions.

- **Sponsored events.** Fewer events, but more budget for each.
- **Field marketing.** Increase "high touch" events in key territories with the greatest concentration of your target accounts.
- **Webinars.** Focus more on internal webinars, leveraging your own database. Third–party webinars are five times more expensive, and have no focus on your target accounts.

- **Advertising.** Higher cost-per-impression, but the same overall budget, or even possibly lower because you're spending money only on your target accounts.
- **Email marketing.** No substantive change.
- **Content syndication.** Higher cost-per-lead, but the same overall budget, or even possibly lower because you're spending money only on leads from your target accounts.
- **Direct mail.** Increase use for "high touch" tactics that capture attention and build relationships.
- **Search engine marketing.** Largely used for competitive blocking tactics, but do not expect much lead generation to come from it from your target accounts.
- **Social media.** Most likely will stay roughly the same. Promoted posts for specific accounts.

3. Engage

Attraction without engagement is just another name for a bounce, so engagement is the next element to create a goal around. One of the main ways to increase engagement is to first do proper segmentation. Do your research to determine what is important to your target accounts: Are they more sensitive to reliability than to price? Do they fall into certain subgroups around doing business multinationally? Do they have taxation as a key driver? For example, some companies may be highly sensitive to tax credits or offshore tax structures, based upon your research.

The old model of engagement involved using broad-brush tactics in the hope that some of those people being attracted would eventually become customers. The ABM approach is to proactively seek these target accounts and put the right messages in front of them to get them to engage with you.

When you test putting different messages in front of these groups based on hypotheses you've developed, you're bound to detect areas that engage much more than others. Your goal is to increase the number and quality of interactions.

Although you can get sophisticated with your segmentation, you may get results with one of the most basic segments of all—using the right industry. One company had target accounts in the automotive, entertainment, hospitality, and consumer goods industries. When they detected that the visitor was from the consumer goods company Zappos, they served up a page with retail messaging and logos from other retailers. When Audi people arrived on the site, they saw automotive-related messages and logos that were congruent with that industry. This approach resulted in a 200 percent increase in white paper downloads. The more relevant your messages are, the more engagement you'll experience.

Don't conclude from this example that you must personalize your site in some fashion for all visitors, because you don't. This is an example in which you can scale the personalization any way you want. At first, do it just for the accounts in your pilot. Be aware that you need to run the personalization on enough accounts for a long enough time that you have reliable statistics. In our experience, companies will end tests prematurely and call them a success or failure before they have a firm statistical basis for doing so. When you can, give the test enough time to run so that you're confident in the results.

Online chat can be an excellent way to engage with prospects. Using the signals generated by ABM, you can configure chat so that if target accounts visit your site, they see a semi-customized invitation to chat.

Let's say that Bank of America is one of your target accounts. You might not want your chat invitation to say "Hello, Bank of America …" even though you could! That may spook people. It may be better to say, "Hello, I'd love to show you how we help financial services companies. Do you have any questions?"

Then again, once a company is a customer and arrives on a page relating to customer support, it may be perfectly appropriate and even impressive to say, "Hi Bank of America, how can I help you today?"

Chat can get even more sophisticated: in addition to the messaging we just mentioned, you can direct the chat sessions to different groups. For example, all prospects that are targets will see the chat and be connected with the sales team. All customers will be connected with the customer success team or with support, and all partners will go right to the channel sales team.

The bottom line here is to make sure your prospects and customers can find what they're looking for, and what interests them the most. Use messaging that reinforces their stage in the sales cycle, or the solution this segment is focused on. This helps to get more target accounts into your funnel to begin with, and it helps to move them through it faster.

4. Convert

The old approach to closing deals was to wait until someone from a target company filled out a form, as a signal—often the earliest signal available at that time—to attempt to close the deal.

With ABM, it's possible to establish conversion goals in which the engagement happens proactively, based on the intent shown by people at the target company. It's powerful when Marketing can pass to Sales a package of signals and intelligence on accounts—information that goes well beyond the simple form-fill and that increases the chances of Sales converting these accounts.

5. Close

Of course, this is the only finish line that you can take to the bank: closed–won accounts. We both know how tough it can be to get to this point in highly competitive environments. That is why ABM is so crucial: having a smaller, defined list of target accounts enables Marketing to apply intelligence-gathering tools to this smaller list. This in turn allows Sales to focus on fewer, higher value accounts and to do so with more information than they had in the past. It's the Adobe example we gave at the beginning of this chapter, but scalable well beyond the 20 or so account plans that could be done manually.

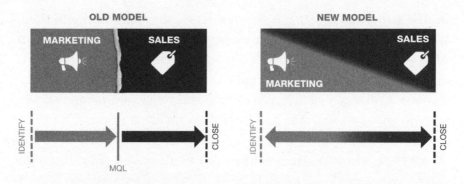

Figure 2.3   Both Marketing and Sales Have Their Specialties, but They Work More Closely in an ABM World

ABM creates a distinct difference at the Close phase, which traditionally was the domain of the Sales team only, as seen on the left portion of Figure 2.3.

Marketing would generate leads, and when they reached MQL stage, Sales would take it from there. Now, both Sales and Marketing work together throughout the entire buying process to help more deals to close, do so more quickly, and also with a higher average deal size, thanks to the focus that the target account list provides.

6. Measure

This is a good time to bring up a fundamental principle of ours: any marketing effort must earn its keep. It needs to show a positive return on investment (ROI) in some form, when compared to alternative methods. We therefore do not suggest that you adopt the ABM strategy because we say so or because lots of major companies use it but because you can document its success in your organization over the course of running a pilot program.

The only way to do such an objective documentation is to establish baselines for your marketing programs by taking a number of measurements. We talk much more in a later chapter about your target account list, but you'll need that before you begin this process. The reason is that you want to continuously measure how your target account list is performing versus non-target accounts.

To set a baseline, look at your current conversion rates and other web metrics like bounce rates, engagement, and so on. Do this for both your target accounts and non-target ones.

The other major benefit of taking these measurements at the outset is that they will help you know what to focus on. For example, ask yourself the following questions about your targets:

- How many of our target companies are visiting our site in the first place?
- Is one of our target industry segments lagging others in regard to visits to our site?
- Are targets visiting, but bouncing in higher numbers, or engaging at lower numbers?
- Are targets currently engaging fairly well, but not converting to leads?
- Based on these measurements, how should we prioritize our efforts?

This brings us back to measuring. Once your originally defined target accounts have had a chance to work their way through the funnel, ask yourself a series of questions:

- What do we see when comparing the performance of those same target accounts before the application of ABM?
- What do we see when comparing the target accounts against non-target accounts?
- How are we tracking to our broader sales and corporate goals?
- How do we prioritize our efforts moving forward? What dials do we need to adjust based upon what we've learned?

This process should make it clearer why you cannot buy yourself an ABM strategy, but you must build it. Every organization is different, so what you need is the data to show that when ABM is applied in your organization, to your type of target accounts, it enables you to move the needle in ways that you couldn't accomplish before ABM.

Heads Up

Another reason why you need the data is that you have some uphill sledding ahead of you to embed ABM fully into your organization. Again, we're just being straight with you here, in this no-BS zone. Any way you look at it, change management is work, even if you have great data to support the change, and even if the change will ultimately be a win/win.

We have Isaac Newton to thank for his concept that a body at rest will tend to stay at rest, and a body in motion will tend to stay in motion. To get some people off dead center and others to move in the right direction, we need all the compelling evidence we can muster, in the form of the measurements listed earlier. We talk in detail in the next chapter about how to get this change to happen in your company.

ABM Maturity Model

Even though you may have never used the ABM strategy in your organization, you fall somewhere on the spectrums identified in Figure 2.4.

Let's look at each of the four areas so you can figure out where you are.

Sales and Marketing Alignment

In this model, the lowest level of alignment between Sales and Marketing is where you both agree in theory about how to work together to achieve the company's goals. You may be thinking that there should be an even lower level, because Sales and Marketing in your organization may in fact not agree in a number of areas. In that case, it's fine to make a note of that situation.

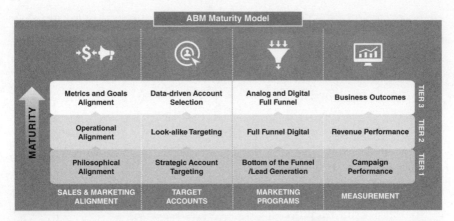

Figure 2.4   The ABM Maturity Model. Currently, Where Are You on It?

One step up in Sales and Marketing alignment is where you not only agree philosophically, but you are working together on a regular basis. This can be easily judged by the level of interaction between the two teams. Are the contacts infrequent and strained, or relatively continuous and helpful?

The highest level is where the teams are working together to such a degree that they're measuring the same things and are ultimately compensated on the same basic elements. There will of course be different compensation details and emphases by department, but goals and incentives should be common, based on revenue, pipeline, and the company's business objectives.

Target Accounts

In proper walk-before-you-run fashion, it's typical for early forms of target account lists to revolve around strategic accounts. They are known quantities and it's an achievement simply for Sales and Marketing to be on the same page about which of these accounts will be targeted.

Up one level of maturity is where target accounts include look-alikes. This is where you know the characteristics of accounts you've been successful at closing, and want to find more companies that exhibit the same profile.

There's also predictive modeling, which focuses on who appears to be good candidates for targeting in the future because they fit the profile well of your buyers.

Finally, there is intent-based targeting, which looks at who is showing buying signals right now.

The most sophisticated models for targeting incorporate all three methods of look-alike, predictive, and intent-based targeting because they will identify accounts that any one targeting method may miss.

For example, if you decided to look only at intent signals, then you would identify only accounts that are starting to do some research on you. You would miss other accounts that may perfectly fit the profile of the types you should be going after, but those accounts are not yet showing signs of intent.

At the early stages of your ABM journey, you may not need to use all three targeting methods because you may have enough target accounts already identified; It's good to know, though, that a combination of these methods is available to identify more accounts when the time comes.

Marketing Programs

The lowest level of maturity is pretty much where many marketing organizations regularly live—at the lead-generation level.

Lead gen is fine for starters, but a level up in sophistication is what we discussed a bit earlier: the ability to apply ABM from the earliest stage in the funnel, in which you measure before, then identify and attract prospects, followed by engagement, conversion, closing, and measurement.

At the middle maturity level, you're using primarily digital marketing methods to accomplish that. The most sophisticated level is where you're agnostic about digital versus analog methods and create a mix that works well for turning prospects into customers and eventually into revenue.

Measurement

Again, the bottom tier of maturity is standard operating practice for most companies—measuring campaign performance.

However, because a campaign can succeed and still be a drain on revenue, the next level focuses on revenue performance. What drives revenue are the measurements of close rates, average deal size, and funnel velocity. Therefore, when the CEO, CRO, and CMO are aligned behind these same business outcomes, they, in turn, will drive revenue.

In your process of determining where your company is on these four aspects of the ABM Maturity Model, it's important to not get tied up in too many details. You may straddle a level in which some aspects are more mature than others. That's fine; mark down your best estimate about where you fall in the spectrum.

The goal is similar to what we talked about earlier: you want to measure beforehand, and then after you've been working your ABM pilot for a while, take another measurement afterward. Not only should that indicate some progress in maturity, it may help to identify areas where you're stuck. These can become priorities for the next period.

Key Transformations of an ABM Strategy

Now that you've had a more in-depth tour of how ABM works, let's review some of the transformations that you'll begin to see as you implement ABM.

Less conflict and more collaboration. Of course, any group of successful people will butt heads on occasion. The problem occurs when that's the order of the day. When measurements, goals, and activities are aligned, you can look forward to the order of the day being working together toward the same end.

Less quantity but more quality. Yes, this can be scary to Sales, which traditionally has wanted leads and more leads. However, the ABM pilot will demonstrate how a sharper focus on quality leads will make life easier for everyone.

Less waste and more efficiency. As we discussed in Chapter 1, no system is perfect but ABM is the best way to put you in the direction of becoming a zero-waste marketing and sales organization. When you mine high-grade ore, there is simply less to throw away.

Less reacting to events and more proactivity. It starts with agreeing ahead of time on the target account list. It continues with optimizing the marketing mix and going after leads higher up in the funnel instead of hoping that some of them will raise their hands through a form-fill.

A focus on insights and not just on leads. As we all know, it's easy to get all the leads you want—just put out a sign for Free Beer. What counts are qualified leads that turn into opportunities, then closed–won business and ultimately revenue. The accelerant that enhances that process is intelligence about your target account list in the form of their behavior and intentions. When people begin to see how ABM provides that intelligence, they need no more persuasion.

~ ~ ~

On the one hand, implementing a comprehensive ABM strategy can be a lot of work. Then again, it's work that is pulling in the same direction, instead of the typical situation in which organizations do a lot of work, but often at cross-purposes.

In the next chapter we discuss how to get buy-in across your organization for a pilot program and eventually for a full implementation of ABM with the full benefits that come along with it.

3

Getting Buy-In

How to Persuade Your Organization to Try ABM

Organizational change.

If you've been in the business world for a while, that term can be enough to send chills up your spine.

When times are tough, the excuse when you try to get people to change is: "Hey, times are tough. It's all we can do to keep the ship afloat, never mind explore new approaches. Let's talk when things are looking up."

Then when business is booming, the excuse for not changing is: "Are you kidding me? We're finally on a roll. In fact, it's all we can do to stay on top of the business that's coming in. We can't afford the time and effort to change horses now. Let's talk when things calm down."

Sound familiar? Yet if you've been in a marketing or sales organization for any length of time, you also know full well how difficult it can be to get things done when people are not only short on time, but have their own agendas. It's natural to wonder: "If sled dogs all seem to be able to pull in the same direction, why can't we?"

What 1878 Can Teach Us

We live in an age of rapid, astonishing technological change. That statement needs no explanation. So in this age of smartphones with computing power that's 120 million times that of the Apollo space-craft computer,[1] exactly what are we doing using a keyboard layout that was designed in 1878?

It sure isn't because it's the most logical layout for a keyboard. It also isn't because the layout has been refined and perfected over 140 years to be the best it can be, which it is not.

We use the QWERTY keyboard because that's what we were taught—and that's what our teachers were taught, and their teachers, too.[2] Besides, it's "not so bad once you get used to it," and lots of business still seems to get done on this ancient layout.

Our point is not to explore the history of typewriters, but to help explain why a clearly inefficient and stagnant mechanism can perpetuate itself with little more justification than "that's how we've always done it. Too much bother to change now."

The Marketing and Sales "Keyboard"

So how has Marketing and Sales always done things? For starters, marketing and sales teams have experienced great difficulty with alignment. Marketing has traditionally had a lead-centric focus, which is pretty much the opposite of their counterparts in Sales, who have always had an account-centric approach.

---

[1] https://www.zmescience.com/research/technology/smartphone-power -compared-to-apollo-432/

[2] Interesting article about how the QWERTY design came to be: https://www. smithsonianmag.com/arts-culture/fact-of-fiction-the-legend-of-the-qwerty -keyboard-49863249/

Then there's the funnel. Marketing usually spends most of their time at the top of the funnel with a quantity strategy. On the other hand, Sales spends their time trying to convert, accelerate, or close accounts that are in the middle or bottom of the funnel.

Because it's historically been Marketing's job to deliver great quantities of leads, the quality has naturally suffered. Then when Sales works those leads and realizes the quality levels of them, frustration and stress between the two teams only grows.

As if that's not enough, there's the disconnect between the measurement systems of the two groups. Marketing tends to focus on granular campaign metrics like butts in seats, clicks, and open rates, when we should be focusing on how our campaigns affect pipeline and revenue.

When Marketing has handed leads to Sales, those leads are typically deemed to be MQLs. Marketing alone is usually responsible for setting the definition of what makes a quality lead. But given that Marketing operates under a quantity mindset—and has also been the one to define what "quality" is, without input from Sales—it's no wonder that tensions run high.

Is there no hope, then? Are we condemned to live on this hamster wheel in the hope that if we just run a little faster, things will change?

No! There's hope. We're not sure how to change the keyboards we all use, but we have in fact seen how ABM can replace the bad old days of traditional marketing and sales.

In Chapter 1, we talked a little about how this is best done: you ease into it. You carefully and gradually make changes so you don't activate the organizational reflex that rejects sudden change. Now let's talk in more detail about what to do and when.

Getting ABM Off the Ground

There is not one perfect sequence of activities to follow because it will depend on the backgrounds and personalities of the people you'll be approaching in addition to the culture of your company.

However, in general, here are the steps to follow, assuming that the people in your organization are at least semi-reasonable but still need some convincing.

Know what the goal is and is not. You are not asking people to "adopt ABM," or "switch to ABM," or "agree that ABM is a better way"—at this stage, all you're going to be asking for is for them to agree to an itty bitty pilot. It should be big enough that you'll get meaningful data from it, but small enough that it doesn't look scary. Just a pilot.

The great thing about a pilot is it can work for two types of people: those who are provisionally behind the idea of ABM will want the pilot, of course. At the same time, there might be people in your company who claim that they "tried ABM and it failed." They may have bought just a tool, given it a half-hearted brief trial, and abandoned it. No matter.

Let's say you have a built-in detractor like this from the get-go. This person may be amenable to the idea of a pilot just to "prove" that ABM won't work in this company, either. Whatever the inclination of these people, the pilot will be a time to find out if those hypotheses are true.

Most people don't necessarily realize that they are frustrated with the status quo because they have nothing to compare it to. They don't know there is a better way. Therefore even if they're frustrated, they may not actively seek substantially different approaches. They work instead to incrementally improve what they've always done in the hope that it will be enough. ABM is not an incremental improvement—it is a seismic shift that improves marketing and sales efficiency, program effectiveness, and revenue.

Be a tester, not a cheerleader. Sometimes the more enthusiastic someone is about a topic the more negative others feel like they need to be. They see you hauling on the tug-of-war rope and find themselves wanting to pull in the other direction. If you are talking with people who have their reservations, then meet them where they are. Agree that we "don't know how this ABM thing will work" in our organization. You might even say that you have some questions or reservations of your own—and that's the very reason why the pilot will settle the matter.

The other reason not to be a cheerleader is you don't want to inject personalities into the decision-making process if you can avoid it. In other words, if ABM is perceived to be "your baby" and "you're sure it will work," then you become too closely tied to it. Better to say that your hypothesis, based on your research, is that ABM may be a way to solve some of the pain points in our current organization.

Identify champions in Sales, Marketing, and Operations. Sure, the ideal situation is an entire unit will be on board with doing an ABM pilot, but that's rare. It's better to assume that you'll need to grow that enthusiasm, by first finding even just one person in each of those areas.

You might be the person from Marketing, but then again, you may be in Sales and want to get your marketing folks on board with finally ending the junk-lead situation and focusing on high-value accounts instead. At any rate, in addition to someone from Marketing and someone from Sales, you need a Marketing Ops person. He or she will be crucial to building your list, and reporting on progress against goals.

The Marketing Ops person often will evaluate, purchase, and implement ABM technologies, once you're out of the pilot. He or she will also connect the business goals to execution. It will involve measuring progress using multiple tools, including web, marketing automation, and your CRM. Having the Marketing Ops person on board from the outset will create a level of ABM familiarity that can accelerate the eventual rollout.

It's important to look for people with that champion mindset—not in the "Olympic champion" sense of the word but in the "willing to try stuff" sense. For every group of people who seem to be stuck in their ways, you usually can find someone who's felt enough organizational pain that he or she is ready for the pain to be over, and thus ready to give ABM a try. It might be a sales rep, or the sales leader for an industry or region.

Identify a few other people with key roles. The following are not necessarily the official job titles for people. We are instead describing the functions that are necessary for someone to do. You need a target account list owner who is the expert on your list. This person knows how the list is put together, who the internal contributors are, and can track performance against the list.

Finally, you'll need an executive sponsor. This crucial person will help guide the necessary alignment between teams, ensuring collaboration and compliance.

We don't mean the legal form of compliance but the group dynamics form. In other words, the sponsor needs to be someone who can assess whether the right behaviors are being shown across the team. Is Marketing still focused on "spray and pray," or is Sales refusing to follow up on campaigns Marketing executes? It may not be much of an issue during the pilot, when people are hand-picked for their willingness to give it a go. People have a way, however, of showing their true colors when under stress, and that will be the situation from time to time.

The sponsor can also help reset expectations. After many years of following the high volume/low quality lead approach, it's a mindset shift to accept lower lead volumes, new roles that come up, and possibly redefined territories on the sales side as a result of this new focus.

It's important to emphasize here that we're not talking about getting budget approval to carve out all these people for ABM. Before you have the proof-of-concept that comes from a pilot, that kind of budget action is a non-starter. The goal, instead, is to borrow pieces of people's time here and there. It's like other projects or task forces that happen from time to time, so that shouldn't be completely new. Keep thinking about a small, temporary pilot, and that will help build the justification for adding this project to people's plates.

Talk with people individually at first. Gather information about where each person's head is in terms of prior experience with ABM, objections, current pain points, and so forth. You'll get better information one-on-one than you will in a group setting, where some of the people you need to hear from may clam up for whatever reason.

Bring out the pain. We know that sounds bad, but then again, we're persuasion professionals. A tested and proven sales principle is "problem agitate solve" and that works on us, too. By getting people to talk about the current difficulties among Marketing and Sales especially, it has the effect of making people understand that you know what they're going through, and that honesty is okay. It builds rapport and further justifies why folks should give ABM a try.

Describe key benefits by department. If you're talking with a marketing person, explain how the ABM pilot has the potential to bring added focus and efficiency. It will also help Marketing be more connected, not to leads, but to revenue.

If the person is from Sales, then discuss how ABM should result in greater precision, coordination, and velocity in target accounts, with focused support from Marketing. Explain how he or she won't have to waste time following up on leads that don't matter.

To someone in Operations, the benefit is at last a coordinated platform and language between Sales and Marketing.

Sooner or later, Finance will get involved. To those people, explain the great news that ABM can bring greater predictability, transparency, and visibility into marketing expense ROI.

Address objections. Of course, you don't have all the answers. Then again, we can provide you with many of the common objections that you'll hear at this stage, and what we've found to be effective responses:

"An ABM strategy sounds like it's going to be really expensive. I don't have the budget for that sort of thing."
Because ABM is an efficient strategy, you can actually engage more of your target accounts on the same budget.

"I'm pretty sure our sales team will not give us their target account list, or work with us to build one."
That may be true, but let's see first if they'll agree for the sake of the pilot, instead of assuming that they won't. Besides, we might be able to find a sales rep or industry team that's willing to work with us on this.

"I'd love to help, but we're already too busy. I just don't see how we're going to be able to implement an ABM strategy."

Because ABM is an efficient strategy with so much less wasted effort, we should be able to actually decrease the number of campaigns and tactics required to reach the same number of pipeline opportunities.

"Let's be real—are you asking us to walk away from the leads that are NOT on our target account list?"

It's true that a certain percentage of our revenue will still come from outside the target account list. It's just that we won't proactively seek them out. For example, if we have a booth at a trade show, then we'll be happy to talk with non-target accounts that approach our booth. What ABM does is focus us on where we can be most effective.

"I'm worried that there will be too few leads for us to hit our pipeline and revenue goals."

What we understand from the experience of others who have implemented ABM is that a properly executed ABM strategy will actually deliver more qualified leads and fewer of the leads that never turn into business.

"Thanks for stopping by. ABM sounds like a great plan for Marketing. Let me know how it goes!"

Well, I'm glad that you think it sounds good. However, ABM needs to be a coordinated program between Marketing and Sales. It's a strategy across departments. For us to realize the greatest gains from ABM, the Sales team needs to collaborate on lists, programs, and messaging.

Remember that many companies have successfully implemented ABM around the world. In the course of your discussions with people, you may run across an objection for which you just don't have an answer. No sweat: if you know some people at companies that have implemented ABM, then ask them. If you don't know anyone at such companies, feel free to contact us, and we'll be happy to give you our two cents on how to answer the question. We do believe we've heard just about every objection under the sun, and have helpful responses for most of them.

Be careful how you ask for commitment. On the one hand, you do want people to lean into this pilot and give it their best effort. On the other hand, asking for "commitment" is fraught with overtones in English: committed relationships are forever and you might hear "Hang on—I thought we were talking about a pilot here! We don't even know if this stuff will work!" Therefore, it may lower the perceived leap to talk about "giving your full support to the pilot." That has no overtones and points to the same goal.

Next Step: Alignment

Once you have your team, it's time to start the process of getting everyone aligned and pulling in the right direction, toward the right goals. How hard can that be, given that we're all on the same team, right?

It's typically very hard to do. It's certainly achievable but we suggest that you don't assume it will be smooth going, or you'll be in for your first wake-up call. There's a concept in psychology called the "narcissism of small differences."[3] It acknowledges that sometimes the groups with the greatest similarities will generate the harshest criticisms of each other. Have you seen that happen? We have.

In other words, if you're in Marketing, expect some of your heaviest lifting to occur within your own department. After all, just within Marketing you have many roles. In fact, depending on the size of the company, there could be 10 people focused on different elements of each of the following areas:

- CMO
- Marketing Operations
- Demand Gen
- Customer Marketing

---

[3] https://en.wikipedia.org/wiki/Narcissism_of_small_differences

- Field Marketing
- Partner Marketing
- Digital Marketing
- Content Marketing
- PR
- Product Marketing
- Industry Marketing

It's extremely difficult to maintain alignment when we all have our eyes on different prizes. Now we're being asked for even more—to see marketing through the ABM lens.

How then, can we hope to be aligned within Marketing, and eventually between Marketing, Sales, and other departments?

What you do is align on goals. To be successful at ABM, you need to start at the big picture with the overarching goals and objectives of the company.

Let's say that a company's primary objective is to increase revenue from the financial services vertical by 20 percent this year. Marketing has an incentive to help Sales hit that 20 percent goal, and each team within Marketing will play a different role in hitting the goal.

So far, this level of goal planning may not be much different from what you are accustomed to. When it becomes different is when you start to connect those goals to the campaigns and activities that will get you to those goals. Take a look at Figure 3.1.

The biggest circle is the Total Addressable Market, or TAM. Because this circle is so large, it's tempting to use it for marketing planning, but focusing on the TAM will yield the lowest conversion rate.

One way to narrow the focus is to think about the kinds of customers you don't want to sell to. If you're a SaaS company, you are likely to know the characteristics of customers that will churn from you within one year. Selling to more of those is in effect losing money on a sale and trying to make it up on volume.

Therefore, when you eliminate those types of accounts, you get down to the next level—the Target Market. They not only fit your customer profile, but you do want them to become customers. What's the problem with just focusing on the Target Market?

Figure 3.1   The different segments of a market

It's the same problem that marketing organizations have struggled with for ages: still too many leads and not enough time or resources to address all of them in a meaningful way. It's also too big of a list for your sales team to focus on. It's indeed true that the world's oceans contain 20 million pounds of gold, just there for the taking. The only problem is the cost to extract it is greater than the value of the gold that can be scooped up in any given operation.[4]

When you take the time to look hard at the Target Market in regard to the accounts that truly are worth pursuing, at last you get to the Target Accounts. It's the list that we will compile in Chapter 4, and the group of accounts that Sales and Marketing will focus all of their outbound efforts on, in order to bring as many of them into the funnel as possible.

Just because you have a target account list, it does not mean that you need to stop there in your segmentation and prioritization. Your account executives no doubt have their most valuable prospects, who represent the greatest revenue potential. These AE Top Accounts are a

[4] https://www.atlasobscura.com/articles/gold-ocean-sea-hoax-science-water-boom-rush-treasure

segment within the target account list, and may well deserve greater attention and resources than other accounts on the target account list.

When Stakeholders Are Not Aligned

Jessica had a workshop to put on and a pipeline goal to hit, and worked with an event planner to make it happen. She got a "good news!" email from the planner, with the message that after just one email blast, the seats for the event were already half full.

Jessica replied: "That's great! How many of the registrants are from our target account list?" Long delay in hearing back, followed by: "Oh; I'll check…."

It turns out that almost none of the registrants were from the target account list. Therefore, after just one email and before the event even began, it would now be impossible to make Jessica's pipeline for the event.

Once you've used whatever qualification methods work for you, then leads become opportunities in the pipeline phase. They warrant extra marketing support in order to maximize the chance of turning into revenue for your company.

Finally, the most precious segment of all are the customers who represent the revenue source for the company. We discuss in a later chapter how an ABM focus can be used to retain and increase the lifetime customer value. You know a lot about your customers. So put that information to good use in marketing programs that help keep them as happy customers.

After Team Alignment Comes Customer Journey Alignment

We both know that the typical B2B sale is long and complex, as shown in Figure 3.2.

The dark squares are the main milestones of the journey, and the light squares are all the other ways we can clarify—or potentially confuse—the situation.

Figure 3.2 Lots of customer touchpoints. The goal is to make them coordinated from the customers' perspective.

It's fine for customers to be exposed to many types of collateral and events. But if all these touches are not coordinated from the perspective of the buyers, it can quickly become confusing to them. A confused mind typically does not buy, but instead delays ("We'll have to think about it"), and delay is the death of a sale.

To ensure that the journey follows a clear path, you have to connect the dots on your touches. That means running cohesive, integrated campaigns. Getting a random direct-mail piece out of nowhere is confusing. But getting a piece about a particular topic after reading an eBook on that topic, followed by a call from an SDR about it, and attending a field-marketing workshop on that topic—that's a journey that may well result in a sale.

Everyone Will Get to Flex Some New Muscles

Marketing must look at their traditional functions through the new lens of ABM. Although it's true that ABM represents an overall paradigm shift in Marketing and elsewhere, it's also true that each area of Marketing will be affected in somewhat different ways because of the different functions.

One shift that will affect most roles within marketing is Sales Enablement. This is a crucial role that traditionally lived with Product Marketing and involved creating pitch decks and competitive intelligence for the sales team. Now, all people in Marketing should wear a sales enablement hat as it relates to their specific roles and the campaigns they execute. If as a marketer, you don't enable the sales team to participate in your campaigns, how do you expect them to succeed? You need to inform them on the goals of the campaign, and the expectations you have of them, as well as what they can expect of you. You must provide messaging templates and calls to action (CTAs) that will help them get meetings. Make it easy for them to access this information as well as lists of accounts included and those that have responded to your campaigns, so that Sales knows where to focus. You also need to clearly communicate your goals and objectives.

Next, think about Demand Generation. Over time, demand marketers have, of course, focused on skills that generate demand—which typically means they sponsor every major industry event, they'll use content syndication vendors to get more names, and will run paid webinars through vendors who bring large audiences.

Now let's use that ABM lens we discussed earlier: ABM-focused demand marketers don't need skills that are only about reach and volume. They instead need skills around how to generate very specific demand from the target account list.

Another example is in Field Marketing. Traditional field marketers have the skills necessary to get their product or service in front of a large number of people in the field. In an ABM world, however, the somewhat different skill is to collaborate with Sales to build programs that get in front of the audience that's most likely to buy and do so in a relevant way. It's also about becoming even more proactive than before.

On the one hand, all of this sounds like work. Fortunately, the payoff comes when all of these specialized marketing functions become more relevant to the target account list and therefore more effective.

Your New Compass Heading

The following eight words sound straightforward enough, but following them is going to require a big shift in mindset, if you're like most companies. Those words are:

A Continuous Focus on
Target Accounts and Revenue

They're easy to say, but actually a challenge to put continuously into practice. The tradition and habit of most organizations is to focus on volume.

Therefore, when it's time to plan the calendar for the upcoming year of trade shows, the old habits will want to kick in.

"I know we're into that ABM stuff but I think it's prudent to play it safe and continue to go to the shows we've always gone to. Kind of belt-and-suspenders style. Then if ABM is showing some promise, we can back off the shows."

The correct response is: "if we are going to succeed at ABM, it will require our singular focus on target accounts and revenue. It's a chicken-and-egg thing. Continuing to do business our old way will not suddenly and automatically produce the results we want with ABM. It will only produce the same old results."

Of course, during the pilot, you will still be doing business the old way and the ABM-pilot way. That's why it is important to configure your pilot using a discrete territory or segment where you can in fact change your planning to reflect the ABM approach.

One company that has had success with ABM is CA Technologies. Erica Short from CA sent us a great visual description of the ABM mindset compared to the traditional one (see Figure 3.3).

The traditional approach to marketing is a lot like the margarita glass: it's really wide at the top and comparatively slimmer at the bottom. The old approach of "keeping our trade show schedule" is

Figure 3.3   Keep this comparison in mind when thinking about ABM

about adding as many leads to the top of the funnel as possible, with very little resulting in closed business at the bottom.

The ABM model of marketing is more like a champagne flute. You put fewer leads at the top of the funnel, but they're higher quality ones. They therefore extend down farther, and result in a fuller pipeline and more closed–won business at the end of the funnel.

Speaking of the end of the funnel, alignment extends to the kind of reporting that ABM requires. First, there are account-based reports that include goals for those accounts, as seen in Figure 3.4.

Then there are other reports that are based on pipeline and revenue, as seen in Figure 3.5.

We go into these reports in detail in Chapter 8. You may have other reports that work better for your organization. However, to be consistent with ABM, they need to be focused on accounts and revenue.

The key to effective reporting in the ABM world is relevance, transparency, and accountability. The relevance part comes from creating reports that focus on accounts and revenue. Then transparency

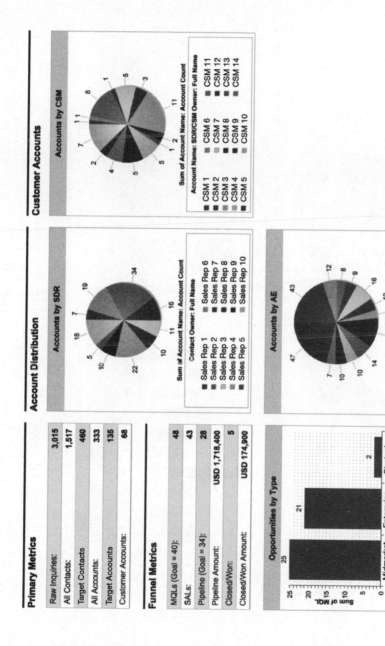

Primary Metrics

Raw Inquiries:	3,015
All Contacts:	1,517
Target Contacts	460
All Accounts:	333
Target Accounts	135
Customer Accounts:	68

Funnel Metrics

MQLs (Goal = 40):	48
SALs:	43
Pipeline (Goal = 34):	28
Pipeline Amount:	USD 1,718,400
Closed/Won:	5
Closed/Won Amount:	USD 174,900

Account Distribution

Accounts by SDR

Sum of Account Name: Account Count
Contact Owner: Full Name
Sales Rep 1, Sales Rep 2, Sales Rep 3, Sales Rep 4, Sales Rep 5, Sales Rep 6, Sales Rep 7, Sales Rep 8, Sales Rep 9, Sales Rep 10

Accounts by AE

Sum of Account Name: Account Count
Account Name: Account Owner: Full Name

Opportunities by Type

Customer Accounts

Accounts by CSM

Sum of Account Name: Account Count
Account Name: SDR/CSM Owner: Full Name
CSM 1, CSM 2, CSM 3, CSM 4, CSM 5, CSM 6, CSM 7, CSM 8, CSM 9, CSM 10, CSM 11, CSM 12, CSM 13, CSM 14

Figure 3.4 Account-based reporting and goals

55

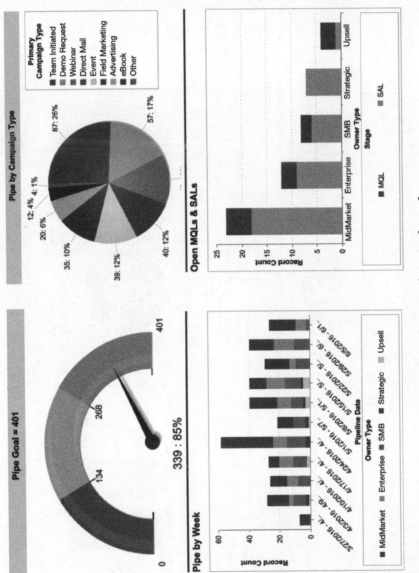

Figure 3.5 Pipeline/revenue-based reporting and goals

and accountability are the result of Sales and Marketing co-creating the reports, meeting together to review them, and holding everyone's feet to the fire.

~ ~ ~

By this point, we have done the substantial work of explaining ABM to various units in the company and we've generated buy-in for the pilot. We also have an idea of how a number of roles and reports will change in order to maximize the chances of the pilot succeeding. Now it's time to tackle the target account list, and that's the topic of the next chapter.

4

Your Target Account List

This List Is at the Very Heart of Your ABM Strategy

By now we've referred to the target account list a lot, and how it is central to any ABM effort. It's now time to do the work of creating the target account list for our pilot.

You should take a bit of care when you choose the name of this list. Yes, you could call it something plain and descriptive, like "target account list," or TAL, but that's missing an opportunity. You are a marketer, after all!

You're taking the first official step in your ABM pilot, and this has the potential to become a turning point for the business, if things go well. Therefore brand your list. This list will be a unifying force in your company—something that will help bring Sales and Marketing together, and it will be the focus of new behaviors across the teams.

At Demandbase, our target account list is called the DB4K, because we currently have around 4,000 accounts on it. Given that your list for now will contain only enough accounts to run a pilot, you may not feel like including a number in there. It could be the Gold List or some other name that works for you.

Beginning the List Process

We carefully chose the preceding words instead of saying "creating your list." To "create" the list can sound like you whip it together and you're done, along the lines of creating a filename. We can assure you that you will not get an acceptable list on the first try, hence our language about beginning the process.

Identify the List Owner

Your crucial first step is to identify this person. (It could be more than one person: in our case, it's a shared responsibility between one member of each of our Sales and Marketing Operations teams, but we'll just refer to the owner in the singular.) This owner is not likely to be the final decision maker for the list. The person you're looking for will end up knowing everything about how the list was created, the criteria involved in selecting the list, where it's located in your various systems, when it gets updated, and so on. This will be your go-to resource for all questions and issues about the list. The list owner has the responsibility for maintaining the list, communicating changes about it, and managing the metrics surrounding the list.

By the way, it's important that there are KPIs around performing the functions we stated earlier. Yes, it's a pilot, and yes, we're scrounging resources from where we can. It would be a potential big blow to the pilot if the list were neglected, inaccurate, and communication broke down. Building in a KPI for this list owner is a way of avoiding the "Hey, I was busy with my day job" excuse for not truly owning the list.

Start Where It's Natural

What's really going to count is the final product—the list that you end up with. What matters less is where you actually start the process, given that lots of people will have a chance to weigh in on the list.

The earliest version of the list could begin in Sales, starting with one or two of your most successful segments. It could start in Marketing if, for example, you earlier identified a champion for this pilot and that person owns a certain segment. Some companies choose to create that first list through team meetings with Marketing, Sales, and Marketing Operations, based on the data in their CRM.

Later, if you like what you see in the pilot and you roll out ABM to the entire organization, you can get sophisticated about list selection, based on data-driven account-selection methodologies and tools that can target ideal customer attributes with intent data. But for now, we're going to take baby steps and begin with our first cut at a list.

As a general rule, you want to have more than a handful of accounts in your pilot, or else you'll limit your ability to show results. Shoot for a pilot with some dozens of accounts. We encourage you to not overshoot and make it too large to begin with. Hundreds of accounts may be stretching it.

Another factor to keep in mind is to begin with the end in mind. Let's think ahead and say you choose a list, get agreement on it, and you end up having what you think was a successful pilot. Let's also assume for a moment that you have some naysayer in your company who seems to enjoy shooting down new approaches. We're sure you have no such people in your organization, right? Anyway, what could this person potentially come back and say about that original list? Could it be shot down because it was highly unrepresentative in some way? Cherry-picked to be a sure-thing success in some way? We don't want to assume that there will be a problem, but then again, it's prudent to step back and see if there are any obvious issues with the pilot list selection.

Therefore, a group of accounts are identified as a starting point, either through collaboration between Sales and Marketing, or through technology, or both. Maybe you even ask more than one pilot-team member to suggest a starting point for the list. You have several ways to think about and segment the list: it can be by industry, company size, geography, product target, customers, or sales stage.

When you get in a room, then ask yourselves the following about the proposed first shot at the list one or more people came up with:

To what extent does this list help us meet revenue goals? You're looking for something that's good but representative. Sure, you could take some of your AE's top accounts, but that might start to look like cherry picking.

Is the list aligned with the company's business objectives? If you build a target account list for a specific region because it needs help achieving their revenue target for the year, but the company is actually divesting itself of that region, the success of your pilot could be moot.

Does the list reflect any strategic initiatives for the company? If so, that's great. If not, it still could be a good list. When possible, align it with a high visibility project. For example, many companies include verticals or industries in their go-to-market approach, so this can often be a good starting point for your target account list.

Is there a positive or negative budget connotation to this list? In other words, it's good to be aware whether these accounts are particularly costly to pursue because of geographical or other reasons. You also don't want non-representative accounts where— as we said before—someone could come back and attack your ROI on the basis of how relatively inexpensive it was to work these accounts.

Does anyone know of any marketplace shifts that may cause us to take an account off the list? There may be a new regulation hitting a particular segment of your list (for example, GDPR) that may have a negative effect on your ability to sell into that segment. By focusing here, you'll be setting yourself up for failure.

What might the Sales rep know about these accounts that could qualify or disqualify them from the list? Your reps should be researching and talking to these accounts on a regular basis. Although as marketers we have a lot of information at our fingertips, we won't know if a sales rep just talked to an account last week and they informed him that they just signed a three-year deal with your competitor.

Does the sales cycle have any implication for the names on this list? These target accounts may be suited for products or services that have significantly different sales cycles. When possible, it's best to choose accounts for which the sales cycle that they're interested in is relatively shorter. That way your pilot can demonstrate results sooner.

Have we chosen accounts that are associated with one product or business unit to start with? If not, it's possible that the pilot could become more cumbersome than necessary. It's best to streamline your efforts here, because you have limited resources (or even "borrowed" resources) to help run your pilot. Therefore, pick a list that has common characteristics so you don't have to create too many variations of your campaigns.

Are there compensation factors involved in the profile of names on this list? Of course, comp plays a big role in any discussion. What we're driving at here is whether we are hampering the pilot by the choice of accounts and their associated compensation potential to sales reps. By the same token, could someone say, "Well it's no wonder that your pilot worked out. Look at the high comp associated with those accounts."

You see the balancing act going on here: sure, we want the pilot to work if feasible for the organization, but we also want the pilot to be reasonably representative of how we would create a target account list if and when we rolled ABM out to the entire company. In our experience, the creation of an appropriate target account list is a significant factor that determines the success of the pilot and of the later full program. It's therefore worth spending the time to build the list with care.

You should also be prepared with a virtual wastebasket handy, so to speak, into which you'll crumple up and toss a number of versions. It's actually a good sign! If your pilot team were not engaged and thought this effort would never amount to anything, then people would shrug and look down at their smartphones during the list discussions. If people are getting into it and going to bat for their choice of accounts on the list, or a particular method they'd like to employ to build the list, more power to them.

> ### Oracle on ABM:
>
> "Like many companies, we segment our market and have a classic pyramid with key accounts at the top and the volume-market toward the bottom.
> We're getting smarter as an organization on using appropriate forms of ABM on that pyramid. ABM can manifest itself in different ways, according to which customers you're trying to reach."
>
> —*Senior Director, Account Based Marketing and Key Accounts*
> *Oracle EMEA Marketing*

Secure Provisional Agreement

Up to this point, only the pilot team is likely to have seen the list. Now you want to bring in the leadership team and others.

We say "provisional" because this is such an iterative process: some decision makers may be uncomfortable with committing to the list before they have every last fact about it. If you encounter this type of pushback, then try to get agreement in principle to the list, and agree also to circle back around when the other factors are known, at which point you get final agreement.

Heads up: don't blast out the list in an email and hope that people will get back to you. We learned the hard way that you'll get much more participation and feedback if you get as many folks in person or on the phone as you can. There are bound to be questions about how you got to this list, why something is or isn't included, and so forth. You don't want puzzled people discussing and concluding things among themselves. Get as many people together or on the phone as you can. Explain how the team has not slapped this list together, but has followed a methodical approach—this would be a good time to list all the questions in the preceding section, relating to how you looked the list over, every which way you could, in your attempt to optimize it.

It's also useful, of course, to say that the list is not perfect, that probably no list can be, and that there may be multiple versions that would suit the pilot, as long as they meet the criteria we described in this section. Then ask if they can see anything that needs adjusting, because you're happy to improve it. That has the effect of softening people who otherwise might be more critical.

Once you've gotten feedback from the leadership team, circulate the list among anyone else who will play a role in the pilot. When in doubt, include people. It's also a way of preempting someone not being included, thinking that he or she should have been, and then that person potentially becomes a critic. Sure, you'll have critics anyway, but some of these steps help minimize them.

Update Your List Regularly

Even though you don't even have your pilot quite off the ground yet, it's time to activate that list owner in order to make sure the target account list is kept as clean as it can be. There will be lots of scrutiny on the list and you don't want to give anyone reasons to poke holes in the pilot. We know that may sound paranoid, but at least in our experience, it's just acknowledging the realities of organizations with lots of strong personalities.

Minor updates to the list will happen on a quarterly basis, and will include things like adding or removing accounts based on territory adjustments, new sales reps, or, hopefully, closing some of those accounts.

There may also be major updates that occur on an annual basis to match corporate goals and objectives. The company may be rolling out a new product that appeals to a new industry or segment, or there may be a shift in focus to go either up market or down market with your product offering. Maybe you've added a strategic accounts team that will most certainly want Marketing's support, and thus will need to be reflected in the target account list.

Part of the pilot process is not just proving the concept, but also putting efficient processes in place. There is no more central process than keeping this list updated, and regularly communicating changes to everyone involved.

Begin to Embed the List in Your Systems

Now that you have your list, it's important to operationalize it across your existing technology stack.

Your target account list will have implications for your marketing automation system, as well as your CRM. These systems are likely to be your first line of communications internally, so it's vital that your target accounts are marked as such.

Next, consider what you'll do about lead routing: which sales reps will be responsible for follow-up on the target accounts. The same goes for lead scoring: if you have a system set up for this, then it's reasonable to factor target accounts favorably into your scoring. By how much? The pilot will help you to calibrate the right score values.

Then it's time to look at your reporting systems. In Chapter 3 we had examples of some dashboard metrics to consider. Now that you have your target account list, the pilot team should pull all the reports that Sales, Marketing, and other departments use to track the degree to which the target accounts turn into revenue.

For purposes of the pilot, put aside reports that will not be affected by these specific accounts; products or regions, for example, that will have no interaction with the target accounts. With the remaining reports, make sure that you'll be able to review results for target accounts versus non-target ones.

Remember that at the outset of the pilot, you must establish a baseline against which the pilot will be measured. Therefore, be sure to pull all reports on the date that corresponds with the launch of pilot activities.

Back to the reports: this new distinction of target accounts versus non-target ones will form the basis for a series of useful questions. For example, when you look at bounce rates and time-on-page measurements, do target accounts differ from non-target ones? How do webinar registrations or white paper downloads differ between target and non-target accounts? You get the idea.

Outbound versus Inbound

We touched on this earlier, but want to visit the topic again: around this point in the pilot, you'll get multiple objections and questions that relate to non-target accounts and revenue. Here are some responses:

"I'm not sure about this ABM stuff because I really need the revenue that non-target accounts provide." You'll still get revenue from your non-target accounts. Even though you'll be focusing on the target accounts, you will still have inbound activities from companies outside your target account list that drive revenue.

"If we eventually move to ABM across the company, are you saying that all my revenue will be coming from this smaller list? Because I don't care how good that list is—I don't see it making up for all the lost revenue from the non-target accounts." Remember that you'll still get revenue from inbound activities with your non-target accounts. But to your point, we're just doing a pilot for now. And part of the pilot process is to assess if we get a higher ROI by applying ABM to this target account list. It may well be that the target accounts will bring in more, if the pilot shows that our close rates are up, average deal size increases, and we have better funnel velocity. Let's find out.

Segmenting Your Target Account List

Even though you're just working the pilot at the moment, it still could be the case that you have different segments represented in the list, although you do want to be mindful of limiting the number here.

Two to three is probably the most you should include. If you haven't already, now is the time to identify them. Then prioritize these segments as a precursor to taking action on them (see Figure 4.1).

Higher priority segments should be relatively small and represent higher potential value to your company. They will therefore warrant a higher share of resources dedicated to winning business. Lower priority segments will still get resources and attention, but at a somewhat lower rate. The lowest-priority segments may receive some resources, but may also just receive little beyond broad-based tactics.

We typically get the following question at this point: *"Hey wait a minute. I thought we had filtered out all the low-grade stuff when we created the target account list. Now you're talking about not focusing much at all on the 'lowest priority accounts' and I'm confused."*

That's a reasonable question, and here's the story. First, creating your target account list is not about handpicking the top accounts in your company. Your account executives have had that sort of list all along. Instead, the target accounts are a mixture of known high-value accounts and the ones that have never had the focus necessary to close them, but it would be great if you could. They may be in a new segment that's just emerging as a focus for your company, or they are potentially great accounts with legendarily tough decision-making processes and have eluded your best efforts to date.

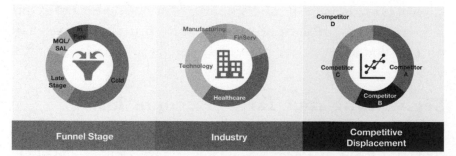

Figure 4.1   The segments you select must have discrete business objectives that Marketing can build programs to support

Second, it's important to remember the word "relative" here. We're simply saying that there are target accounts and non-target ones. Then within the target accounts, there are further distinctions and segments to be aware of. The target account list is not one monolithic blob of accounts with one profile.

Some of the lower priority accounts within the target account list might be great candidates for one-to-few or one-to-many marketing methods. In that case, they require relatively fewer resources but still represent good revenue potential.

Therefore, within the target account list, make note of those higher- and lower-priority segments by thinking about the following factors:

- The account's revenue potential for the company
- The attractiveness of the company to help you secure other, similar companies
- The propensity to buy, based on current business or personal relationships, customer satisfaction scores, active investment in competing or complementary products or solutions, and the win/loss ratio from previous sales cycles
- How well your current sales team is organized to handle the account in regard to personalized attention

In Chapter 2, we discussed how your marketing mix will change in an ABM context, with certain methods being trimmed or eliminated, and others gaining in focus and resource allocation. Now that we have the target account list in hand, we can take that analysis one step further: we can look at the account prioritization and then start to think through how each segment within the target account list will be exposed to which marketing methods, and when.

We're not creating a Swiss watch here, where it's possible to be painstakingly precise about every gear in its exact place. Instead, we're working with a vastly more complex set of moving parts—accounts, segments, industries, tools, and most complex of all—people.

Therefore, you will not get this planning perfectly right. That's okay. By doing this level of coordination between the teams in your company, your target account list, and the sales and marketing methods, you'll be vastly increasing the chances of delivering more revenue from the effort.

Set Your Goals

After you create segments in your target account list, it's time to establish goals and objectives for those segments. Here are some good examples of objectives:

- Increase funnel velocity for late-stage accounts by 15 percent
- Increase revenue from a particular industry by 10 percent
- Win at least three customers of our competitor, Acme Industries

Naturally, given the limited scope of the pilot, the goals need to be calibrated accordingly. It may even be that it's only at this stage of setting goals for segments within your target account list that you decide that it would be better to swap out some accounts. If doing so will make the goals clearer, then that's an example of good iteration. Especially when you're setting up the target account list for the first time, it's important to anticipate and allow some modifications like this as everyone works through the new process.

Expanding Your Target Account List

Of course you'll be growing your target account list if the pilot is successful and you're now scaling it up. But what about growing it during the pilot?

During the Pilot Period

Under the right circumstances, that's okay as long as you're careful about it. If you realize early on as you create your first target account list that it would be more logical to expand it, then it could make sense, for example, to include a whole territory instead of a piece of one. Just guard against expanding it based on initial excitement with the potential of ABM to the point at which the list has grown beyond the resources you have available for the pilot.

Let's say you're well into the pilot, which is coming along nicely, and people are making noises about wanting to expand it. Aside from the issue of overrunning your resources, there's another consideration, relating to test methodology: if you add accounts partway through, now you won't be comparing apples to apples—target accounts to non-target ones. You'll instead have some that have only recently been added, and that group will throw off your numbers because they cannot be at the same stage in the sales cycle as ones that have been worked for a longer time. In short, don't do it.

Down the Road: Ways to Expand Your Target Account List

When you're out of the pilot and are looking to expand the target account list, there may be less need for proof-of-concept, although it will still be important to recognize the apples-to-oranges issue.

When you are ready to grow the list, you have some options. The first is to scale it horizontally. You might expand to include a new business unit, other product lines, different teams, or segments.

The other approach is to scale vertically by going deeper into your segments to expand within a segment that has already shown success. It should still include the original companies on your target account list minus those that you have now sold to. But with your new knowledge about these segments, you'll now include additional accounts to go after.

At Demandbase, we built our first full target account list by identifying some commonalities among our best customers. We then sought out more companies with those same characteristics. That list contained about 1,500 accounts, divided among 12 sales reps.

The following year, our sales team had grown, as had our revenue targets, so it was time to grow our list. We brought on a predictive-analytics tool to help us identify the next best set of accounts to add to our list. We didn't want to dilute the success of our ABM strategy, so more data was required to ensure the integrity of our list. The tool leveraged our CRM data about the accounts we had in our database. It then generated a list that eventually became roughly double the earlier size, to accommodate a large increase in our sales team.

There is a third method, known as intent-based. It's even more sophisticated and combines ideal customer attributes with intent data from across the Internet and first-party data (that is, data you directly collect). This method can identify new accounts to go after as well as the most likely buyers within those accounts. You can also have the accounts ranked by their propensity to buy from you.

We generally see companies build their ABM systems using the look-alike method early on. Then as they become more sophisticated and active with ABM, they are in the best position to benefit from the predictive method. In Chapter 11, we review how various models— look-alike, predictive, and intent-based—can work together to identify your ideal account list.

How Big Should My List Ultimately Be?

As with lots of good questions, sometimes the only accurate answer is, "It depends," because businesses are so different. However, here are some things to consider:

Think about your total addressable market. Next, that list will get filtered by the accounts that are actually ready to buy now and are not locked into other contracts or are not in play for some other reason.

Then consider the length of your sales cycle: the longer the cycle, the fewer accounts you'll have per rep. That's because the reps must follow their respective target accounts through a lengthy buyer's journey that requires more time and attention by reps.

Of course, you must also take into account the size of your sales team. If you have only 20 sales reps, and the target account list could potentially have 20,000 accounts, that would be far too many for each rep to handle.

Finally, consider your close rates: the higher the rate, the fewer accounts you'll need per rep. If close rates are low, then reps will need more accounts to get to the target revenue number.

We developed a model to help you figure out the different factors that affect the size of your list and apply them to your own business to determine how big your list should be. It's shown in Figure 4.2.

If you would like a copy of this model in Microsoft Excel format, please contact us at ABMbook@demandbase.com and we'll be happy to send it to you.

Customers, Partners, and Your Target Account List

We've discussed prospects a lot, in regard to how they fit into your target account list. But customers and partners are two other stakeholders that should figure prominently in your target account list, especially after you're out of your pilot and looking to expand (see Figure 4.3).

In later chapters, we cover how you should tune your messages to different prospects within your target account list based on their verticals and other characteristics. Let's now discuss how you can market to your customers and prospects more efficiently using ABM.

	MIDMARKET		ENTERPRISE	
	PRODUCT 1	PRODUCT 2	PRODUCT 1	PRODUCT 2
ANNUAL Quota per rep	700,000	300,000	1,200,000	800,000
% of Quota coming from TAL	0.75	0.75	0.75	0.75
Average Deal Size	95,000	65,000	175,000	145,000
# of Closed/Won per rep from TAL	5.5	3.5	5.1	4.1
Close Rate	0.2	0.25	0.20	0.30
Total # of Pipeline Opportunities Req'd	27.6	13.8	25.7	13.8
% Conversion of TAL to Pipeline	0.30	0.30	0.35	0.35
Total Accounts Needed	92.1	46.2	73.5	39.4
TOTAL New Business TAL per rep	138.3		112.9	
# of Reps	12		15	
Total Target Accounts needed (TAL)	1659		1693	
Total TAL (MidMarket & Enterprise)	3352			

Figure 4.2 These factors help determine the size of your target account list (TAL)

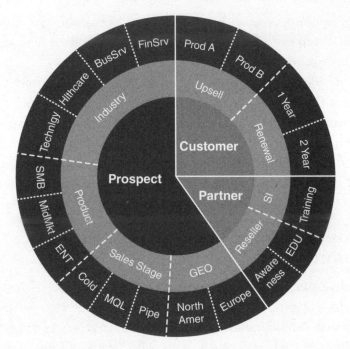

Figure 4.3   The eventual elements of your target account list

How ABM Helps You Market to Existing Customers

For many newer, or high-growth companies, the focus of their ABM efforts will be on generating new business from net new prospects. But for many companies—especially ones with a large installed base of current customers—most of their revenue will come from retaining and upselling those customers. At Demandbase, most of the companies using our technology typically include some combination of prospects and current customers in their target account list.

The great news is that you're even more likely to have success with customer marketing, and here's why: with prospect marketing, you need to make a number of assumptions. However, you know a good deal more about your customers—what they've bought; what their renewal cycle is; you have an account manager who's talking to them on a regular basis; you understand their specific business challenges; and so on. This means that you should have a really good idea about the next appropriate product or service that your company should sell to them.

It therefore becomes pretty easy to segment them and make sure that you're getting the exact right message in front of them at the exact right time.

Be careful, however: even though you have all of this information, don't try to sell customers on the next suitable product for them on the day after they sign a contract. You want them to use and appreciate the product you just sold them. Make sure they have the support they need to be successful, from the products or services they just purchased from you. That will put them in the position of asking you what else you have rather than feeling like they're in a cycle of continuously being sold something.

Therefore, focus on support and education right after their last purchase. Let the account team stay close to the customer and understand where they are and what they need. Then, when the account team gives you the green light for the renewal and for the upsell, that's the time to change your targeted marketing to begin discussing the next logical product for this customer. This will support your account team to help make that upsell a reality.

Let ABM Transform Your Partner Marketing

It goes by lots of different terms: partner marketing, channel marketing, channel sales, or strategic alliances. Whatever the name, this has traditionally been an area with great promise, but great frustration, too.

First, the promise: If you and another company have complementary products and services, and both serve the B2B market, then you potentially have a win/win. You can co-host events, for example, with each of you inviting guests, and each of you splitting the costs of the event. That not only takes some of the pressure off each company to fill the entire event, but it also means each company has the potential to bring in new accounts from the other company's list as well as both of you marketing to greenfield opportunities.

Now the frustration: First, it's traditionally been extremely hard to quantify and prove the ROI of partner marketing. Second, if both organizations have a lead-volume approach, then the problems inherent in that model are just multiplied by two. If Marketing and Sales don't much talk to each other within a company, then coordinating Marketing and Sales between two companies just adds to the potential for disarray. Sure, some business may come from the event, but it's much more hit-or-miss, depending on who shows.

Another problem is, let's say we're hosting a VIP dinner. Without a defined target account list, organizations tend to fill the seats with anyone they can to satisfy their commitment to fill half the seats. That sometimes results in attracting lower-level folks from not-interesting accounts, who think: "Sweet! A free dinner at a fancy restaurant? I'm in!" Not good for the ROI.

Here's what ABM brings to the table: If you've found that ABM has helped to provide focus for your organization internally, then ABM can provide a similar focus in your partner relationships from both a marketing and sales perspective, if the same principles are applied.

We mentioned earlier the issue of attracting non-ideal accounts and people to events. That doesn't happen when the two partners establish a joint target account list for the event in which all accounts are of interest to both companies. If some of the accounts are already customers of one of the partners, it provides a soft intro to the second partner. The ABM approach means you end up with an event in which everyone in the room is valuable to both partners —a very unusual situation, indeed, without ABM.

But what about if one company is on board with ABM and the other is not? In our experience, in partner marketing, one company tends to be the big dog. If the little dog is using ABM and the big dog is not, that's a problem. But if the big dog is the one onboard with ABM, then this can work well. The big dog simply lays out the plan of how the target account list will be co-created, what the marketing mix will look like, details of the campaign, and so on, with some input from the little dog.

When you are jointly marketing to the co-created target account list, there's another hidden benefit. Often, the two companies may have the same account in their CRM. But the two companies had previously developed relationships with different people within that account. The joint marketing uncovers some of these additional decision makers at each company.

By the way, based on our experience, we recommend that you develop a target account list that is three times the size of the event.

Proving the ROI becomes much easier with ABM because you can say: "We identified these 30 accounts that we were going to work on together with the other company. We were able to bring 55 percent of them into pipeline and closed 48 percent of those." ABM provides a much clearer line of sight to the actual impact it's having on the business.

The 30–60–90–Day Plan

We've covered a lot of material, and that can sometimes become confusing in regard to just what happens when. It's therefore helpful to look at your pilot in terms of what should get accomplished in the first 30, 60, and 90 days, as seen in Figure 4.4.

First 30 Days

The good news is if you've done the steps we've described so far in this book, you're well on your way to accomplishing the milestones listed under the first 30 days.

You know your champions and the other members of the pilot team. You have secured the necessary resources to conduct the pilot and have created the target account list. You've also met individually with team members and have had some team meetings as well.

	FIRST 30 DAYS	FIRST 60 DAYS	FIRST 90 DAYS
Philosophical Alignment	Identify your Champions. Agree on business objectives of the strategy.	Establish the roles and responsibilities required for a successful ABM plan.	Communicated out to the affected Sales & Marketing teams.
Target Account List	Identify area(s) of focus • How big should your list be? • How much of Marketing's resources will be focused here?	Establish Segmentation Strategy. • What are the business objectives for each segment?	Figure out how often to review/iterate on your list.
Planning/Review Cadence	Host initial meetings w/ABM Leadership Team.	Establish a regular meeting cadence.	Work with Marketing to conceive of programs to achieve these objectives.
Setting Core Objectives	Benchmark current metrics: • Average Deal Size • Sales Velocity • Close Rates	Establish improvement objectives with ABM strategy.	Socialize with everyone & Marketing.

Figure 4.4   Sales and marketing alignment activities in the first 90 days of your ABM pilot

You've taken baseline measurements of current deal size, sales velocity, and close rates in addition to interim metrics like target account list engagement, penetration, and pipeline conversion rates to use when assessing the pilot later.

First 60 Days

In this period, you'll continue to refine the roles and responsibilities. You'll focus a lot on refining the segmentation of the list and aligning the marketing mix to those segments. You'll also begin to set goals for improving how ABM is working in your company.

By 90 Days

By this point everyone in the company may have heard something about ABM, and certainly the Sales and Marketing teams will have seen it in action in their jobs, or will have been briefed on how the pilot is progressing.

This is also when you'll begin to think post-pilot, and how to plan for a larger rollout. Don't be alarmed if you read this and think: "There's no way my company will ever move this fast!" Rather than thinking about it in days, think about it as Phase One, Phase Two, and Phase Three. But don't let these phases linger: if it will be more than 30 days per phase, establish the length of each phase at the outset. Otherwise, your pilot could get stuck in a phase for too long, and the pilot might lose steam or even die altogether.

~ ~ ~

You have accomplished a lot to get to this point. Not only have you sold the idea of a pilot, you've organized a team to execute on the pilot. You have also done the hard work of creating and refining your target account list.

Even so, you're not quite ready to go all-out with the pilot. We've talked a little about measurements, but in the next chapter, it's time to get detailed goals, measurements, and dashboards set up.

5

Attracting Your Target Accounts

How ABM Turbo-Charges Your Ability to Attract Accounts

We know our target account list, and that means we've built our first of six pillars of ABM—"Identify." Now it's time to target those target accounts, so to speak, by using marketing methods that are tailored to be most effective.

There's a science and little bit of an art that goes into the process of attracting your target accounts. It's largely the job of the demand-gen team, and it's a combination of different methods to capture the attention of the target accounts. ABM enables the demand-gen folks to spend their money more wisely because of the highly specific list of accounts they are going after.

Some of these methods are online and digital, but others are offline and low-tech. Both the high-tech and low-tech methods can be effective if they're executed properly. We review many of them in this chapter and how they're best put to use in conjunction with ABM.

Marketing Automation Systems

You most likely had been using a MAS before you found out about ABM. If you haven't, they are tools that maintain the marketing database, launch and manage email campaigns, and provide analytics into marketing performance. Some MA systems are sophisticated, with the ability to create campaigns using visual drag-and-drop tools.

It's possible to have a highly sophisticated MAS—which is a technology platform—but get little return on your investment if that MAS is not coupled with the focus that the ABM strategy provides. You can automate your marketing all day long, but if it's spray-and-pray marketing that is done with the traditional mindset of "volume is king," then in our opinion you will have automated the wrong thing—you'll have become efficient without being effective.

ABM brings to the table the high-resolution targeting of accounts you care about. It also lays out the principles and practices you need to align Sales with Marketing and other units of your company. Most important, ABM—if implemented properly—aligns those units along the dimensions of accounts and revenue.

Account-Based Advertising

Almost every company with whom we meet tells us that they have a top-of-funnel challenge. In other words, they're not attracting enough of their prospects to engage with them. That's why advertising is one of the most common tactics used. But traditional advertising has always had a specific challenge: you may have heard the quote attributed to John Wanamaker, who built a department store empire in the late 1800s: "Half the money I spend on advertising is wasted. The trouble is I don't know which half."[1] If Mr. Wanamaker

---

[1] https://en.wikipedia.org/wiki/John_Wanamaker

were alive today and using account-based advertising, he would know that both halves of his advertising budget were working for him.

Account-based advertising allows you to target the delivery of ads to different types of audiences. You can:

- Deliver an ad to anyone who's identified as being from the target company.
- Constrain the delivery to people who are likely to be on the buying committee for that company.
- Focus the delivery on an individual.

Those are the people who will receive the message. Then there are the tuning options for the message itself. It's now possible to target the message so it refers to any known attribute about the account: company name, industry, location, relevant product, case study, or call to action.

Think how these types of personalization stand out among a sea of general messages—and completely irrelevant ones.

Don't be surprised when you implement account-based advertising, and your cost per impression goes up. That is offset by the fact that your overall budget may go down because your spend is so targeted. You won't be paying for impressions that go to companies outside your target account list.

The Economics of Account-Based Advertising

Let's look at the economics of account-based advertising when compared with traditional digital advertising. With the traditional approach, you purchase ads from publishers or through public exchanges. Let's say you spend $50 K per quarter, for a total yearly spend of $200 K. You get 17 million impressions for your money, and some of those impressions reach your target accounts. In fact, about 15 percent of them result in target account engagement.

With account based advertising, you get to target ads to specific companies across all networks. You'll spend about $30K per quarter, or $120K for the year. That will generate about eight million impressions, but once again, all from your target accounts.

Here's where it gets especially good: your target accounts get engaged at a 25 percent rate, and it took fewer impressions to do the job. Figure 5.1 summarizes the drop in spend and increase in target account engagement. Of course, these are not formal projections, but instead the sort of results we've seen companies achieve with ABM.

At Demandbase, we eat our own dog food. In other words, we experiment on ourselves to validate our hypotheses. Common sense is very useful, but it's even better to have data on test results when possible.

In the case of one test, our hypothesis was the following: "Accounts who receive our ads are more aware of Demandbase, and those who receive our ads and who engage on our website are more likely to turn into pipeline."

We then designed an experiment to test this hypothesis. We took our target account list and delivered personalized ads to them, in

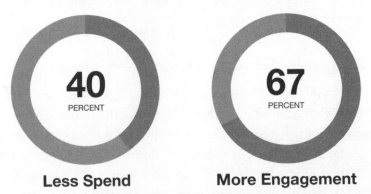

TARGET ACCOUNTS ENGAGED

40 PERCENT

67 PERCENT

Less Spend   **More Engagement**

Figure 5.1   The effect that account-based advertising can have on your digital-ad budget

Figure 5.2   We used a variety of ad personalizations to get accounts to engage

which the goal was to get them to engage with our website regardless of whether they clicked on the ads or just typed our URL into a browser. Our evaluation period was two quarters.

In Figure 5.2, you can see the types of ads we ran.

Our metric was pipeline generation rate. We established a baseline rate of target accounts engaging with our site before we ever delivered these ads to them. Then we ran the ad campaign.

What we found was that the accounts that engaged more with our website as a result of our ad campaign were 60 percent more likely to turn into sales opportunities than the accounts that didn't engage more than the baseline amount.

We know what you are probably thinking: *big deal—of course, accounts that are more engaged as a result of ads are more likely to convert to a sales conversation. They are by definition the active ones.*

Demandbase sells to marketing organizations, so it seems like the website cmo.com would be a really good place to advertise. Although we were getting to VP and C-level marketers, 95 percent of the visitors on that site weren't on our target account list. In other words, we had 95 percent waste from advertising on that website. (Some other company might have only 15 percent, depending on its target account list and other factors.) We decided to use our own Targeting Solution ABM platform and invested in advertising that would serve ads only to accounts on the target account list. It is now a zero-waste advertising strategy.

But here's the cool part: ABM and account-based advertising allow us to identify those target accounts that engaged on our site as a result of our ads. We couldn't do that before, unless they filled out a form. Now we can detect the engagement of those specific accounts and create a campaign just for them. They're the easiest accounts to sell to, judging by the 60 percent increase in conversion opportunities.

You may wonder: "How is engagement a better metric than the common and popular one of click-through rate (CTR)?" It's true that many buyers will click on ads at some point, and tracking clicks is not useless. It can be a directional indicator of engagement levels, especially in the short term. However, the CTR metric is not very useful to compare one ad against another because it's blind to who may be liking one ad over another.

In contrast, when we combine ABM with company-data-enhanced website analytics, not only can we observe behavior and engagement of visitors without their ever clicking, but we can know how much of that behavior is from our target accounts.

One of your early tasks should be to explore all the possibilities before you, as it relates to account-based advertising. First, establish which of your target accounts are currently engaging with you. Are they coming to your site, or engaging in some other way?

Next, armed with that information, develop a list of possible strategies to attract those target accounts that are not currently engaging. During the pilot—when you probably have not invested in much ABM technology—you still can make progress here. You can manually personalize direct mail, for example. Looking back at Figure 5.1, you could have pieces that personalize by a specific product, or by the target company's size, or by some attribute of the account like geography. You can also target your field marketing and event strategy to maximize their effectiveness with your target accounts, which we discuss later in this chapter.

It's work, but it's a pilot, and you're laying the proof-based groundwork that down the road can form the basis for getting a platform that will automate these processes, as well as give you other capabilities.

Case Study: Progress

Progress.com offers its customers a platform for building and deploying applications quickly and easily. They provide a range of services to 140,000 companies, including the likes of Coca-Cola and Toyota.

To generate awareness around their new brand and to position themselves as a thought leader, Progress originally implemented a traditional online advertising campaign. Although the campaign performed reasonably well, Progress noticed that specific companies from their target account list were not responding to their ads. To solve this problem, they decided to try ABM and started with a pilot.

Progress established three goals for its ABM effort:

1. Attract the right accounts at scale and with a limited budget
2. Engage visitors even though the majority of visitors were unknown
3. Accelerate prospects to revenue

To prove the concept, Progress focused on one key industry—Consumer Goods. They targeted approximately 200 companies within that industry. They then personalized the messaging to speak directly to the Consumer Goods audience on both the ad and the corresponding landing page and on the home page.

The Progress team personalized various aspects of the pages to align with the target audience. Their personalization focus was the hero image, headline, body copy, and customers showcased. The goal was to drive users deeper into the site, so the metric chosen was "next page clicks."

For certain interior pages, other personalization included displaying relevant success stories and messages relating to each visitor's industry. It was also possible to prioritize the solutions featured on the product pages to be most relevant to a visitor's industry. On these pages, they used the metrics of pages per session and exit rate to assess the level of engagement.

Progress also focused on live chat and on forms. When a chat user from a target account was recognized, Progress delivered a personalized message plus a photo and contact information for their account executive.

Forms also benefited from ABM. Because a lot of firmographic information was already known about target accounts through the Demandbase ABM account-identification solution, Progress could significantly reduce the number of fields on their forms. In some cases, they chose to prepopulate the form with information.

Progress was able to benefit from a significant lift in attraction, engagement, and conversion of its target-account audience.

What About Retargeting?

For some years, one form of retargeting has been popular in the B2C world. In this form, advertisers would detect that a consumer had searched for "Barbados hotels," for example. Then when that consumer went to a news site, blog, or many other websites, she would see display ads for hotels in Barbados. The concept is to keep that thought on the top of the consumer's mind, until she hopefully pulls the trigger and books that vacation.

That may sometimes work in the B2C world, but it becomes inefficient and costly for B2B purposes if it's not modified through the use of ABM. Here's why.

Most B2B websites get loads of traffic of all types, and most of those visitors are not from companies that will buy from you. Only a sliver of that traffic is from those targeted companies—typically less than 15 percent. At the same time, some of your visitors are also your employees and vendors. If you use the traditional broad brush to retarget all those people with display ads, you're throwing away the majority of your retargeting spend.

For retargeting to be effective in the B2B world, it must be account based. That means the retargeting ads will be shown only to people from the companies on your target account list.

There's another benefit to ABM-based retargeting, as shown in Figure 5.3.

With the long buying process that is often the case in B2B, some of your target companies may go for weeks or even months without activity on your site. By the time they do show up, there may be only a short period to influence their decisions.

Monitor candidate accounts ▸ Capture active buying signals ▸ Identify highly engaged accounts ▸ Re-target engaged accounts with personalized ads

Figure 5.3   A way to retarget with less waste and greater effectiveness

When someone from a target company does appear on your site, you can detect different buying signals based upon behavior. Then you show relevant messages to that person. You can also activate retargeting for the extended stakeholder group from that company. Not only does this allow you to tune your retargeting dollars to the companies you care about, but the personalized messaging has the potential to move customers more quickly to conversion.

Mini-Case Study: DocuSign

You may have used DocuSign as a consumer when you were involved in a real estate transaction or filled out other agreements online. They're the leader in e-Signature transaction management.

Even though DocuSign's users may be individuals, their business is B2B: they negotiate agreements with large companies that have many thousands of contracts and other documents to be signed electronically.

DocuSign became interested in ABM because they wanted to create a personalized digital experience for segments within their target account list.

Their list focused on six industries. Their goal was to create personalized advertising through the entire customer life cycle. They used ABM methods to launch separate company-specific digital campaigns for those six industries. It was a combination of

(continued)

Mini-Case Study: DocuSign *(cont'd)*

personalized targeted ads, driving individuals in those companies to personalized website content.

This level of personalization had the following results:

- Bounce rate decreased from an average of 35.5 percent to 13.5 percent

- Page views went up by more than 300 percent

- Average time onsite increased by more than eight minutes

- The sales pipeline for these six industries grew by 22 percent

Field Marketing

All ABM-related methods do not have to be digital for attracting your target accounts, and field marketing is a good example.

Field Marketing takes on different forms, depending on a company's needs. Sometimes it's a regional events team or a target account team that works with the most valuable accounts.

Regardless of the particular flavor, Field Marketing often takes on a reactive role, helping out when the sales team asks it to. Although that can work, it sometimes does not result in a consistent focus on the most-important accounts for the company.

Here's how to apply ABM to Field Marketing: first, map where your target accounts are located around the United States and elsewhere. Then find the areas of greatest concentration; it's often major metropolitan areas, but there may be a different distribution.

The next step is to review the resources you have available in the form of budget and head count for Field Marketing. Then get Field Marketing together with Marketing and Sales and come to an agreement about how many cities you can reasonably cover. Remember that all areas need not be covered alike: you may agree that some of the biggest opportunities should receive Strategic Account focus, along with more resources.

Approaching Field Marketing planning this way will benefit you in three ways:

1. They'll enjoy alignment with Sales as they work, quarter after quarter, to satisfy the needs of pipeline generation and acceleration.
2. Field Marketing will become a regular presence within these cities, and that will generate its own momentum.
3. When new sales reps come into a territory, Field Marketing will be able to get them up to speed much more quickly, given that they know the territory, the accounts in play, the pipeline, and they have programs ready to execute.

Can this level of alignment and planning be so new to some people that they resist or return to their old ways? It happens. Additional training may be necessary, or even hiring different types of marketers. But these transitional pains should be easily offset by higher close rates and improved sales velocity.

Other Best Practices in Field Marketing

As you know from reading this far in the book, one of the key principles of ABM is for Sales and Marketing to be aligned. One of the best ways of doing that is to have individuals in Field Marketing make one-to-one connections with people in Sales, in the form of shadowing.

In other words, the field marketer every so often is included on sales calls, to see exactly the dynamics on the ground. The shadowing can also take the form of attending meetings, either as a silent observer or active participant—whatever the two people agree on.

We have seen this practice work extremely well, resulting in better marketing, informed by first-hand interactions with customers, and also better working relationships between the two teams.

Another best practice is to support what might be called DIY projects in Sales. Even if Sales and Marketing have a great working relationship, you may agree that there are always some spontaneous or non-budgeted sales ideas that aren't quite ready for prime time, even though they look promising.

In these cases, Marketing agrees to apply the 80/20 Principle and offer roughly 20 percent of normal marketing support in the hope that these side projects might achieve 80 percent of their desired outcome.

This will usually take the form of providing solid marketing discipline to an Account Executive's fledgling idea in such a way that the ROI can be determined at the end of the project. We've found that some of these side projects don't work out—to no one's great surprise—but that others turn out very well, and then become part of the official Field Marketing roster.

Getting Social

Your social media manager has an opportunity to work closely and effectively with Field Marketing and Sales, and here's how. At Demandbase, our field marketing team runs targeted campaigns in specific regions. They'll work with Sales and the social media unit to do online research about target accounts as it relates to decision makers and their social media presence. Then our social media manager or sometimes the field marketing person will tweet at a target prospect with relevant messaging and content.

The goal is not to get likes, retweets, and comments, though that sometimes happens. The real goal is to be able to walk into a meeting with people at the target account and be able to establish rapport quickly, based on interests gleaned from social media.

One of our AEs had 20 target companies in a territory. We were able to launch a field campaign that included social engagement from 14 of the 20 accounts. The AE reported back that the conversations with those accounts were unusually cordial as a result of the social touch.

Your Event Strategy

When we speak at conferences, we will often ask for a show of hands: "How many of you think you do *too many* events?" We can count on at least half the room to have hands raised.

The reality is most marketers would like to sponsor fewer events, but it's much easier said than done, especially in the non-ABM world. There, where volume is king, it's hard to turn down the prospect of getting another batch of leads.

Fear of Missing Out, or FOMO, happens in other ways, too. We know our competition will be there, so how would it look for us to be absent? Will that start the rumor mill? We have also been going to that event for 10 years straight, and besides—some of the people there are among the nicest.

Those are reasons just on the marketing side. When you factor in all the events that Sales asks for—well, it's for all these reasons that so many hands go up after our question.

The great thing about ABM is it gives you a framework for determining which events to sponsor, and how much to invest. It also is a planning mechanism that is objective and defensible.

It starts with having your target account list. Then look at last year's events and determine which ones produced the most pipeline. The goal is to figure out what made those events successful.

A central question to answer is: What percentage of attendees are on your target account list? You'll likely find that there is some percentage of target accounts, below which your events have diminishing returns.

Next, have a discussion with others on your team—people who are also veterans of these events. What factors contribute to your most successful events? Is it sometimes a particular sponsorship level? Is having a speaking slot important? How about workshop sessions? Ask the same question about executive briefings, client dinners, sponsored outings, and other activities at events. You'll probably come to the conclusion that some of the events you've done in the past don't make the cut. On the other hand, you may conclude that certain events have lots of potential, but may cost a little more in order to maximize their effect.

You won't extract all insights in just one analysis session, but after that first one, you'll be much farther down the road at understanding what might make for a successful event in regard to moving target accounts along in the buying journey.

Then, when your Sales team or executives come to you with suggestions for events, you have some specific data and criteria with which to evaluate those suggestions.

This is a process that's helped marketers not only be seen as more collaborative by their sales teams, but also to trim events that just don't make the grade. Not only does that allow you to free up time and budget for other programs with greater potential to reach your target accounts, but your sales team can spend less time at these so-so events and more time in their territories, selling.

Keep in mind that ABM changes two things about events: first, it most likely will change which ones you'll invest in, as we discussed here and in Chapter 2; second, it changes the event activities. It's a focus on target account engagement rather than booth leads. Instead of handing out fancy swag and rolling out that margarita cart at happy hour, you'll invest in a private room for one-on-one meetings with target accounts, and maybe also do a VIP dinner for them.

Webinars

As you probably know, webinars are powerful marketing tools. They can be live events, or recorded and replayed. They allow for real-time interaction and for screen sharing, all without the requirement of travel.

It's common for B2B marketers to work with publishers to produce thought-leadership webinars as a way of generating leads. If you're implementing an ABM strategy, we suggest you instead produce your webinars in-house and market them directly to your target account list. In-house webinars are far less expensive, and because you're marketing to people already in your database, they are warm and more likely to convert. If you're looking for net new names for your database, there are more effective and targeted methods, like content syndication.

There's a hidden bonus to producing your own webinars: you get the registration and attendee lists in real time, which you can then immediately share with your inside sales team. At Demandbase, we generate about 30 percent of our opportunities from webinars *before the webinar date.* If you don't get this list until after the webinar, you're missing an opportunity. One trade-off about producing webinars in-house is that you'll need to subscribe to a webinar-hosting platform. They are sophisticated tools, but still have more of a learning curve than outsourcing the whole thing. You'll also need to create your own webinar content and invite your own guests, but we think it's a small compromise for a large potential return.

Content Marketing

According to Google, YouTube is the second-most-visited destination for business-related searches after Google itself.[2] When you consider that 75 percent of Fortune 500 executives view videos online, and 65 percent of senior executives have visited a vendor's site after watching a video—it's clear that video has a place in content marketing.[3]

YouTube alone has 300 hours of video being uploaded every single minute, and 5 billion videos watched every day—and it's just one video provider.

Video is just one way to deliver content. We are all awash in content: in a single minute, more than two million new WordPress posts are created, 215 million new emails are sent, and—you get the idea.[4]

Content is exploding because there's an appetite for it. However, we also know how challenging it can be to find useful information among the torrent of junk.

How can we as marketers cope? How can we stand out from the crowd? One solution is the focus that comes from ABM.

As with other attraction methods we've discussed so far, the first step is to have your target account list. The simple fact of knowing whom you're trying to target is huge.

---

[2] https://cdn2.hubspot.net/hub/139831/file-17772438-pdf/docs/bestpracyou-tube.pdf?t=1535403315793

[3] https://www.smamarketing.net/blog/b2b-youtube

[4] http://videonitch.com/2017/12/13/36-mind-blowing-youtube-facts-figures-statistics-2017-re-post/

Next, segment your list to make sure you're providing a relevant message to each account. If you're doing this for the first time because you're in the pilot phase, then you may not have many segments. Later, when your target account list does cover many segments, then choose a small number to start with.

Now it's time to get with your customer-facing teams like AEs, SDRs, Customer Success Managers (CSMs), plus folks from Field Marketing and Demand Gen. That will represent a great deal of knowledge in the room or on the phone. You know whom you're targeting, and also what segments they represent. Now the questions are:

- What are the needs of these target accounts?
- What challenges are they currently facing?
- How do they consume content?
- What types of content do they prefer?
- What types of personas make up the buying committee?
- How are decisions made?
- What information do we have about advisors or thought leaders that the decision makers trust?

If you get answers like "it depends," then that may mean you need to segment further, until you're dealing with a group of accounts with which people in the room can feel confident about the answers to the preceding questions. You therefore might focus on a couple of verticals, or one industry, or a particular sales stage.

Then again, if you get a lot of puzzled looks, it would be better to start with accounts where this sort of information is known. That will also buy time for people to get the information on accounts where it is missing.

With all the information you have now assembled, it's time to compare it against your existing inventory of content. Some pieces will be a clear match, others will be semi-relevant and still others will be not relevant to a given segment of your target accounts. Use a spreadsheet to match your content to your handpicked segments of target accounts.

Next, add some descriptors next to the content pieces.

Top of the funnel (ToFu): These are content pieces that represent thought leadership in the form of blog posts, books, eBooks, videos, infographics, and so on. It is important material to persuade B2B prospects, but it's also the most abstract and big-picture focused.

Middle of the funnel (MoFu): This level includes case studies, white papers, and product-focused collateral. The content might take the form of PDFs, webinars, email sequences, and so on.

Bottom of the funnel (BoFu): As the name implies, materials at the BoFu level are pretty product-specific, like free trials, pitch decks, product-specific handbooks, and so on. They can also come in the form of printed material, PDFs, and webinars.

When you're done with this inventory, each piece of material on the spreadsheet inventory will indicate the relevant segmentation as well as where in the funnel it should be used. You should also add to the spreadsheet which target accounts are suited to receive each piece.

After this process, you should have a good idea about what exists and what holes you'll need to fill with new content. Depending on the audience you're targeting, you may be able to take existing pieces and tailor them to fit particular segments. It's even possible to keep the piece as-is, and make the landing page be more specific to the segment with relevant logos, imagery, and copy.

In Figure 5.4, you see examples of simply changing the cover (and a few interior references) of the same document, with the version on the left side targeting the financial services industry.

At this stage, you'll know what content truly does not exist and must be created. As you should do with events and field marketing, make the target account list your guide about which pieces of new content should be prioritized over others.

For example, let's say you're a bit light on event coverage of a given group of target accounts, relative to other groups. You may be able to counterbalance that by creating additional content for that group.

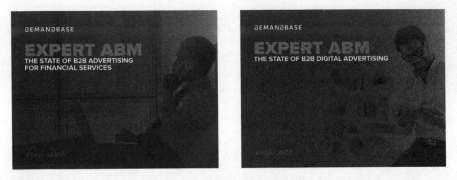

Figure 5.4   Same piece + simple changes = targeted piece

Once you know what you have and what you'll soon create, then it's time to build a distribution plan. Together with Sales, look at your target account segments and plan how all the content will get in front of an audience. You might send some material directly to accounts. Other pieces get delivered by email, or at events. Still other pieces can be used on pages of your website that get customized on the fly, depending on whether a certain target account is viewing it.

As we are fond of saying, ABM is a team sport. By having teams across Sales and Marketing collaborate on what needs to be created, and how it should be delivered to whom, you're helping to knit that alignment even closer together.

How do you judge the success of your content marketing? It's fine to start with some traditional measures like number of downloads, page views, and social media mentions, as long as you are comparing those measurements by target versus non-target accounts. You may have an asset that has the most downloads you've ever seen, but if only 5 percent of the downloads come from your target account list, was it really a success? On the flip side, you could have an asset that got 10 percent fewer downloads overall, but your target accounts represented 90 percent of the downloads. In an ABM world, the lower overall number of downloads is less important than the degree to which the asset resonated with your target accounts.

The best practice is to add some measurements that more fully describe what is going on in your funnel, as shown in Figure 5.5.

Measurement Across the Funnel

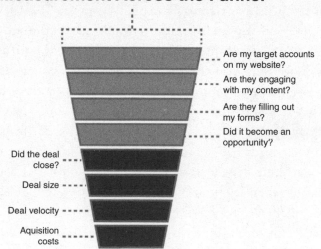

Figure 5.5   **Traditional measurements are fine for top-of-funnel, but you need other measurements to see the whole picture**

You'll need to lean on your CRM to help get these MoFu and BoFu measures, all the way from MQL to SAL to pipeline opportunities and then closed revenue.

Maybe you won't have your reporting all set up early on, but that's another reason to have a pilot. You'll be getting all of this in place, so by the time you want to scale, you'll have the systems in place to handle it.

Defining Your Initial ABM Attraction Strategy

We've discussed several methods to attract your target accounts. In fact, we've covered enough ground that you're possibly not sure where to start.

To address that, think about what your key challenges are at the moment, as it relates to your funnel.

You may feel like it's a ToFu issue, in which your company is not getting the visibility and brand recognition it needs. You may find yourself having to cover the basics with prospects about where your company is positioned in your industry.

If there is this lack of awareness, or misconceptions, then that's a reason to ramp up your content marketing at the ToFu level. As we discussed, it may not even require entirely new content. The very process of doing the content inventory may make you realize that you have more than you thought. In that case, it's an issue of being proactive and making it more visible through content syndication, or account-based advertising.

Then again, you may feel like the weakest link is at the MoFu level, in which your leads have converted to opportunities, but they seem to be stalling there. If you have data about which target accounts are getting stalled, then it could be time to revisit your Field Marketing and event plans. What activities are planned where these accounts are located? This might be an area in which you don't have the right content to help these accounts stay engaged, or the right content is buried on your site four-clicks deep. What intelligence does Sales have about objections and misconceptions relating to these accounts? Might that give you clues about changes you could make?

What should you do if the issue is more at the BoFu stage? ABM focuses on target accounts, and it also focuses resources on accounts that are farther along in the funnel. The solution may lie in shifting your ABM emphasis for these accounts to more of a one-to-one or one-to-few approach, to see whether this higher level of personalization and attention may get them over the finish line.

~ ~ ~

No matter what you conclude, it's still early in the ABM process. You've identified your target account list and we have discussed several ways to attract these quality accounts in a way that traditional methods cannot, at least at scale. We discuss in the next chapter how to engage these accounts using the powerful methods available within ABM.

6 | Boosting Engagement

Practical Steps You Can Take to Keep Accounts on Your Website

It's certainly critical to identify your target accounts and then attract them. Equally critical is engagement, because attraction only serves to open the conversation. Engagement is the engine that moves people through the buyer's journey until they eventually, we hope, buy. Central to the discussion of engagement is segmentation and campaign integration: instead of delivering a one-size-fits-all message, you want to make sure that whatever channel prospects use to engage with you, they will receive a consistent message that's relevant to them.

We all have seen the statistics that tell us how many thousands of advertising messages we're exposed to every day. Though the numbers are going to vary greatly, we can agree that it's a lot. And that's just advertising, never mind news, blogs, and so on.

As a result of this Niagara Falls of information that we're exposed to every day, we use an unconscious process literally within a handful of seconds after arriving on a website. Researchers crunched more than two billion data points and concluded that you get the thumbs up or thumbs down within about 10 seconds.[1] Of course, a website is only one of many engagement tools at your disposal. But because it's the one that every decision maker will interact with, it is worth your while to make it as persuasive as possible.

Let's say we're searching for a new hosting provider for our company. When we type in "hosting" and land on a page, the clock is running as we instantaneously do a form of pattern recognition: "Is this what I expected?"

To put it another way, your first sale is 10 seconds long, and it needs to show different segments of your audience that you have what they need. To be clear, you're not closing them on your product; you are instead closing them on the relevance of your site to what they're searching for. One study found that 60 percent of B2B website visitors left after looking at only one page.[2]

The Net and the Dart

As consumers and B2B customers ourselves, we know how poorly most sites perform at this instantaneous sale. Most sites follow conventional wisdom of casting a wide net. It's spray-and-pray again: *"Let's load our home page up with all our products and services to all our audiences. That way, something is sure to stick."*

Meanwhile, at the very time that companies are trying to cast the widest of nets, the potential customers are using what might be considered a dart—a sharp, narrow search for just the thing they want.

Why is the search so narrow? Because many stakeholders, especially in B2B sales, have the luxury of being able to do a great deal of research while remaining anonymous. They review blogs, LinkedIn, articles, and forum threads with peers. By the time they get to a company's website, they know what they're looking for, as shown in Figure 6.1.

---

[1] https://www.nngroup.com/articles/how-long-do-users-stay-on-web-pages/
[2] The study was conducted by GoTranspose.com and involved a survey of B2B companies.

Figure 6.1 **By the time prospects are on your site, they've formed a lot of opinions**

Most companies are using a wide net, and most prospects are throwing narrow darts that fly right through the net.

Segmentation changes all that. When you tune your message to a narrow market, and make it abundantly clear on your home page—or on landing pages, if that's where visitors get sent to—then you transform a wide net into a fine sieve and capture the attention of those visitors.

Personalize the Message

Once you've segmented your accounts into groups that share some common characteristics, then you can increase engagement through personalization.

But first things first: we now live in the ABM world, and that means we must tie personalization back to business objectives. Here are some examples:

1. Increase revenue by 15 percent from a particular segment
2. Win four customers of Competitor A
3. Increase revenue from our existing customers by 20 percent

When we use the word "personalization" it can sound like we mean it only in the same sense as a personalized letter with someone's name on it. However, there's a whole spectrum of personalization options open to you.

4. Name of the company visiting your site
5. Name of the industry the company is in
6. One product line or service
7. Even more specific: a single product, model, or service
8. Geographic location
9. Size of company
10. Industry association that the company is affiliated with
11. Common "enemy" (for example, government regulation, disruptive competitor, foreign power, and so on.)

You may be asking yourself: "Do I need to personalize every piece of content for every target account?" No, that's not where we're going. We suggest that you start small, with just the companies in your target account list pilot, or even a subset of those. Then merchandise your existing content to those segments in a meaningful and relevant way, with tailored messages using one or more of the options on the list.

As we mentioned in Chapter 2, Adobe used personalized logos and references to four different industries. These were not separate sites or pages, but the same page that was personalized in real time for these four industries. Visitors from other industries saw a generic version of the page. The personalization resulted in more than a 200 percent increase in white paper downloads (see Figure 6.2).

Another interesting fact about this personalization was that the white paper was the same for all four very different industries. In personalizing the content around that white paper, they were able to grab the attention of that visitor because they established relevance up front.

Another example of personalization is using a company name and discount program the company uses in ads and on a website (see Figure 6.3).

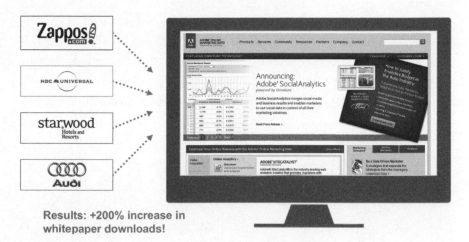

Figure 6.2 Personalizing by logo and specific industry

Don't Assume the Delivery Medium

Another way to match your message to your audience and increase engagement is by experimenting with different delivery mechanisms of that message.

For example, you may have a text-heavy page that does a good job of describing your service. It is worth testing that very same message, but in video format. Some people learn best by reading and others would much rather watch a video. The extremely popular "TED" series of presentations acknowledges this fact: visitors can watch the TED Talk or read the transcript of it.

Figure 6.3 Personalizing by company name can be powerful

Another medium to consider are podcasts, which at least by one measure are overtaking blogs in popularity.[3] They're allowing podcast publishers to reach audiences when they otherwise may not be accessing any other media; for example, while driving or working out.

Amazon repurposes the same book in eBook, printed book, and audiobook form to reach the widest audience with the same message. Although some of these media may be used in B2C transactions, they are not limited to B2C.

Live Chat, Turbocharged

Once you get people to your site, they're only engaged if they are finding what they need. You can accomplish that through personalization of the home page, having clear navigation, and a search capability so people can type in their request instead of hunt for the relevant pages.

Live chat solutions, if implemented well, can enhance engagement even further. It's one thing for me to type in a search query and be served up results that may or may not be relevant. It's another to be able to ask a real person on the other end of the chat window, and have that person help curate a solution.

Many companies have used chat only as a support or customer-service tool. When you know which company is visiting your site, however, you can choose to show and personalize the chat or not. For example, you might show it only to target accounts and keep it off for non-target ones. It's a far more effective use of this powerful tool.

Adobe wanted to enhance its existing live chat by adding ABM capabilities. When that was done, then the live chat system was able to identify the company a visitor was coming from in real time. It then delivered critical firmographic data like company size, industry, and location to Adobe chat reps. Here is how Adobe described it:

> Knowing what company you are about to chat with is incredibly powerful from an engagement perspective. When you have more context, you can steer the conversation in a direction that leads to a larger opportunity.[4]

[3] https://www.searchenginejournal.com/podcasts/261447/
[4] Quoting Thomas Gadd, *Account Development,* Adobe.

ABM-enabled live chat delivered further benefits. Because Adobe was able to know the company and key attributes of the person they were engaging with, it could route visitors to chat agents who were best suited to answer their questions. The chat agents had greater visitor context, which meant more-effective conversations. As a result, chat-to-lead conversions increased by around 200 percent.

Leverage Data

Dive into the data from your marketing platforms and website analytics to understand your visitors' characteristics and intentions. Based upon that data, what assets (white papers, webinars, events, and so on) are relevant to your target audiences? This can help you to drive them to the right content and ultimately increase conversions. It will also help you understand what sorts of assets you should be proactively pushing out to those same segments.

Always-On Advertising Increases Engagement Across the Buying Journey

In Figure 6.1, we talked about how prospects can form opinions long before they visit your site. That's all the more reason to reach out to them using account-based advertising, as we discussed in Chapter 5.

However, the greatest effectiveness occurs not only when you're contacting them earlier in the buyer's journey, but when you deliver a consistent and personalized message throughout that journey.

That brings us to another best practice, which is that your B2B advertising should always be on in order to fully engage prospects. Again, if you look at Figure 6.1 you see that prospects have a long period of engaging with a topic before they typically engage with a solution provider by visiting a site, filling out a form, or calling the company.

Always-on advertising delivers three benefits to you:

First, it ensures that you're getting your message in front of key decision makers at a target account. Because we're usually talking about several decision makers, the reality is that they may separately be at different stages of understanding the options and solutions out there. Having your advertising on at all times and at different stages of the funnel means they start to receive a consistent experience and message as they move through that funnel.

Second, always-on advertising gives you better visibility on the progress of accounts. As a prospect moves along the journey, ideally you want to have access to data and buying signals that provide insights about how to move prospects along to the next stage of the funnel.

The third benefit is data-related: the longer you have targeted advertising running, the better data you have on your prospects' behaviors. For example, you can begin to understand any patterns in engagement among the accounts that eventually close. It allows you to keep getting better over time.

To get the most value from always-on advertising, make sure you also have continuous tracking of website engagement.

Seven Steps to Phasing in Website Personalization

Fortunately, integrating web personalization is not like leaping to a new CRM or accounting system. You can personalize as gradually as you wish if you follow these seven steps:

Step 1: Audit your website content. Conduct an inventory of the content you already have. As we said earlier, the problem is often not a lack of content, but instead a one-size-fits-all approach to delivering it. Review your material like case studies, webinars, and other content with an eye toward which segments could use what content. Some content may need slight personalization, but that's pretty fast when compared with creating new content from scratch.

Step 2: Identify high value pages. All pages are not created equal, and they certainly don't all perform equally well. Use your analytics package to determine the pages that get the most engagement, and that are the most common pages to be visited before buying signals like filling out a form, calling Sales, watching a demo, or visiting a pricing page. These should be your initial personalization pages. It's also a good idea to personalize the home page because it typically gets a lot of initial traffic and creates strong first impressions.

Step 3: Measure and analyze. Go beyond traditional measurements like clicks and page views. Instead, look at each key target account and segment their analytics, measuring how they are behaving on your site.

Step 4: Identify quick wins. If you want to start personalizing content right away, you can begin by tweaking CTAs, which are things like "submit" buttons. You can also tailor website headlines and images to appeal to certain segments. It's even possible to use the same piece of content for multiple segments, as long as the surrounding message is personalized.

Step 5: Create the personalization variations. Especially if you're just getting started with personalization, it's worth keeping things simple and orderly. Create a spreadsheet or other repository once you have identified simple things to personalize on a site (you can later get as sophisticated as you wish), for example, logos, testimonials, industry-specific videos, background images, headlines, subheads, and CTAs. Then for each segment, industry, company, or other way you will personalize, write the copy, gather the images, get the logos, and so forth. At first, just personalize for one target account so you get the process down. Soon you'll be able to scale it rapidly.

Step 6: Drive traffic to your personalized pages. To do the A/B testing that we talk about in step 7, you will first need sufficient traffic to see statistically significant results. By syncing your personalization efforts with your demand-gen team, your personalized pages can get more traffic sooner. That coordination can also help to deliver consistent messages from advertising, email, and social media to your personalized pages.

Step 7: Optimize and repeat. Optimization is a critical component of your website personalization strategy. Conduct A/B tests to see which variations work best for a given element. For example, if you're focused on showing different industry-specific logos of companies using your services, run a test to see if just the act of showing different logos has an effect on conversions. We discuss this process more in Chapter 7.

~ ~ ~

If you apply just a fraction of the methods we've discussed in this chapter, the level of engagement shown by your target account is bound to increase—substantially. Fortunately, you don't have to take that on faith because your pilot project will produce the data.

Of course, visitors who engage all day long are great, but what's greater is when they raise their hands to take things to the next level. That's the topic of the next chapter.

7

Converting and Closing

If You Can't Close Them, Nothing Else Matters

The B2C world certainly has its challenges, but in a number of ways, the grass is greener with the B2C sale.

Take conversions, for example. You send out an email with a seasonal sale notice, and drive people to your site. They enter a promo code and some of them buy. The end result is usually considered to be a conversion in the B2C world, although certain other actions like form-fills or webinar registrations can be counted as conversions as well. At any rate, relatively speaking, B2C funnels are shorter, include vastly fewer decision makers, and do not include the concept of "opportunities."

When it comes to B2B, however, conversions are not the point at which the figurative cash register rings. Instead it's when customers raise their hands by filling out a form, calling Sales, registering for a webinar, and so on. The whole substantial process is unique to the B2B world of MQLs turning into SALs, some of which turn into opportunities.

Signals and the Buying Journey

Engineers like to talk about signals and noise, and it's easy to see a good example with an old-school analog radio: as you move the dial, most of the time all you hear is static. Suddenly, you stumble on clear voices broadcasting the useful signal.

B2B marketers spend just as much time as engineers doing two things: creating an environment in which the most signals are generated, and then trying to separate the signal from the noise.

And there is a lot of noise. When are prospects even prospects? It's certain that some of the traffic to your site is composed of bots, students doing research papers, your competitors, journalists, and so on. Let's therefore examine a series of signal elements, what they mean, and how to influence them.

The Changing Mix of Buying Signals

Not all buying signals are going to be as overt as a form fill or a chat engagement. Also, not all signals are created equal. Look at this example of the average buyer's journey for the 12 months leading up to an MQL (see Figure 7.1).

The shades in each stack represent the different channels: events, webinars, form fills, demo requests, and field-marketing touches. Different channels are engaging with accounts at different points in the buying cycle.

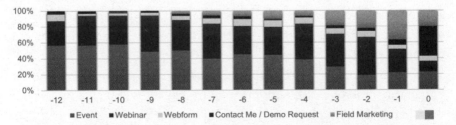

Figure 7.1   As the months progress, the mix of signals changes

Earlier on in the buying cycle, you see people choosing to be a little more self-serve by engaging with webinars and downloading eBooks. Right before an opportunity, they tend to go more to field-marketing events or fill out forms so they can be contacted.

When you measure and analyze these trends over time for your organization, you begin know what are reliable indicators of buying behavior, and you can share and prioritize that with your sales team. From a marketing perspective, you can design programs to address and capitalize on these signals in a meaningful way in order to help get these accounts into closed–won status.

Another signal that is really important to share with your sales team is website traffic. Understanding the increase in web traffic month over month, what sections of the site they are visiting and the number of unique visitors will help identify accounts that are heading into a decision-making process. On the other hand, if your rep is already engaged with an account, but their website traffic plummets, that might signal that the account is in jeopardy of being lost. It's time to contact Sales and see if they can get feedback on the account.

That accomplishes two things: it may salvage an account that otherwise may be wandering away. It can also provide feedback over time from Sales to Marketing about whether that was a reliable signal or a false alarm. Another example of doing granular analysis in order to get better over time.

Heat Maps Deliver Insights

There is now a class of tool that gives you the potential to learn a great deal about visitors who land on a page, and it's almost a little spooky. Research shows that to some degree, eye movement and mouse or cursor movements are positively correlated.[1] You may know this intuitively if you think about where you hover your mouse as you go through a webpage.

---

[1] https://static.googleusercontent.com/media/research.google.com/en//pubs/archive/40760.pdf

These tools can record every mouse movement and click, overlaid on the page where it is happening. Then you're able to call up a recording and see precisely where an individual clicked or hovered, and then which pages that person went to next, or pages returned to for further reading. It's called "heat map analysis" because it shows lots of clicks as a red area, and very few clicks in green or another color.

This analysis gives you a pretty good idea of content that visitors focus on, and content they're ignoring. For example, there's a concept in conversion optimization known as a "false bottom." This is where a page is designed in such a way that many visitors don't even realize that there's more to see if they were to scroll down. They arrive, look, and leave. The recording tool will indicate if any scrolling took place. By detecting this behavior and then redesigning the page by moving a few elements around, you can determine if you get deeper engagement on the page and whether conversions increase because visitors now see a form or other CTA lower down.

Another benefit from heat maps is the ability to detect page elements that are effectively invisible. Let's say you use ABM tools to insert logos in a certain area, but you also have a compelling image lower down on the page. Heat map analysis will show you whether people's eyes immediately jump down to the image and don't even focus on the dynamically inserted, relevant logos. Heat maps are a great way to give people what they are after, when they want it.

As is the case with other forms of analytics, it's important to distinguish between the behaviors of your target accounts versus everyone else. In general, customers or engaged prospects are after different things on your website when compared to casual visitors, competitors, and others. The best insights come from segmenting first, and only then analyzing behavior.

On-Page Signals to Watch for

Because ABM allows you to focus on the behavior of target accounts on your site, you're already down the road in terms of filtering out a lot of noise. Even so, behavior on websites can sometimes look puzzling or random. Here are a number of potential signals to pay attention to:

Returning to a page many times. Although visitors may naturally do this with home pages, it could be more of a signal when the page is dedicated to one of many products you offer.

Search terms entered. Most sites have search tools in the upper right area of at least some pages. However, in our experience, most companies do not analyze visitor search queries for clues. If you do so, you may detect buying signals in the form of queries that take the form of "Product X versus Product Y," "Product Y refund policy," or "Product X API." The latter could indicate that the visitor is interested in Product X, especially if it has an Application Programming Interface to other systems.

This level of information is actionable in two ways: First, it allows Sales to contact the account and answer some of these questions. Second, it allows you to see the very information that visitors to your site are looking for. Especially for target accounts, it's important that they find relevant answers. We all know what it's like to use a search tool and be told "0 results to your query." Worse yet are results that get served, but are irrelevant to the query. By examining search logs, you can determine how many searches resulted in poor or nonexistent answers, and fix that situation for future visitors.

Visits to the pricing page. This is a useful signal to analyze, especially in conjunction with a heat map, with which you can see the features they hover over and click on.

When you have multiple subscription levels or options, it can be helpful to have a feature that lets people select the options they're interested in and have the page do a side-by-side comparison. It might be comparing the "Platinum" versus "Enterprise" option of a product, and that should give Sales an idea of what to discuss with the account.

What precedes action. Does this account visit the pricing page immediately after watching a demo? That may be an indication that the visitor likes what he or she sees and the issue now is price. If the pricing page is visited immediately before someone does a form-fill or calls Sales, that would be another positive signal. In contrast, visiting the pricing page and then immediately exiting the site would be a reason to believe that, at least for now, price is a significant objection.

FAQ section. A package like Google Analytics will tell you that someone visited your FAQ page, but stronger insights come from what that person does on the page. It's useful to have the FAQ in the form of an "accordion" in which the question is shown and when the visitor clicks on the question, the answer opens up beneath it. Not only does this make for a compact page that's easy for visitors to scan, but your heat map application can then show you the specific questions that the visitor wanted answers to. If you couple that analysis with what the visitor did next, that's powerful.

For example, let's say the visitor opened a section about your Service Level Agreement regarding 24/7/365 support, and then immediately went to schedule a demo, or call Sales. That would be a strong buying signal.

With all the signals we discuss here, just make sure that you base your conclusions on looking at your target account's behavior—and even segments within those accounts—and not on visitors as a whole.

The Great Gate Debate

Recently, more and more B2B marketers have begun to move away from putting everything behind forms, and instead to leave much of their content "ungated." Marketers have realized that many B2B buyers prefer to remain anonymous when they're evaluating purchasing options. As a result, they'll often choose to not download content if they must fill out a form with their contact information.

Savvy B2B marketers are picking up on that. Especially for an account-based approach, you want as many people as possible within an account to consume your content. Therefore, eBooks, white papers, and videos are becoming more commonly ungated.

Other high-value content, like webinars, continue to remain gated. For those cases, here are a few best practices for maximizing conversions.

The web form is a tried-and-true demand-gen tool. However, studies have shown that the longer the form, the less likely visitors are to fill it out, even if the content they're after is useful to them. You have a couple of options for reducing that friction.

First, think hard about the amount of information you ask for, especially for first-time visitors. Sometimes companies will load up a form with information that ultimately would be useful to have, but it puts off visitors. For example, asking for a phone number too early will cause many people either to leave it blank, put in a fake number, or abandon the form. Later in the funnel such a request will cause no friction at all.

The same is true for form fields that ask about annual revenue, number of employees, and so forth. For the very first contact, see if keeping it to a minimum will increase form completions: name, email, and company. We talk in a later chapter about tools that can append information about the company, removing the need for many form fields.

After you've minimized the information you request on a form, you may increase conversions even further by spreading the form out onto two dialog boxes. The first box might just ask for email. That's a great first field because—unlike name or company—the email is something you can use to get back in touch with the visitor, even if that person leaves right after providing it.

Filling out that one field is so quick and easy that many people will do so without much pause. Then the next dialog box might ask for another small amount of information, sometimes in conjunction with useful information on the page like testimonials, or other product information.

It's also a good idea to have a mention of privacy beneath the "submit" button on a form. Even though we're discussing B2B transactions, decision makers in companies want to know that their information will be kept confidential.

Ways to Increase the Likelihood of a Conversion

Let's look at several aspects of a B2B sale as it relates to your website, and how to maximize the chances of turning a lead into an opportunity.

Pricing Pages

We discussed earlier how it's important to know what happens after someone visits a pricing page. Now let's discuss the page itself. An important principle to keep in mind is: don't make them work.

If you have more than one product offering on the page, then organize it so people can compare apples to apples. It's common to see a product with many features listed beneath the prices. It's best to line up the features across products so people can quickly tell what the higher levels of price will get them. As common sense as this sounds, it's not something that some companies do.

Also, when listing features, be careful not to assume too much technical knowledge. Yes, it's a B2B sale, and some of the decision makers may have technical jobs, but the CFO and other senior people may not. Therefore, the best practice is to list technical specifications if necessary, but to have tooltips or links to where some of these details are described.

It's a best practice to reinforce the value of the product or service on the pricing page. It may be that the first visit by a target account will be to your site and quickly to the pricing page. Not only should the main aspects of your value proposition be stated—or restated—on the pricing page, they should be reinforced with customer logos relevant to the target account. The probability of a conversion can be further enhanced by displaying testimonials from other customers in the same segment as the target account.

If your products or services include any form of guarantees, then they should be conspicuous on the pricing page.

Discussing the Competition

A core principle of ABM is that the earlier you can reach target accounts in the decision-making process, the greater your chances of turning them into customers. Two of the earliest questions on the mind of potential buyers is, "Who offers what I need?" and "How do they differ?"

Does your website address those fundamental questions? Many B2B sites do not, but if you think about it, by addressing them you become genuinely helpful to buyers in their journey to making a decision.

You can address the first question without directly listing your competitors. Instead, let's say you offer a highly rated SaaS solution. You could make a prominent mention somewhere that your solution is reviewed by G2 Crowd, and is also part of a Forrester Research report or a Gartner report. That's furthering your goal while being helpful at the same time.

The second question was, "How do the solution providers differ?" That will also be addressed in reports from Forrester and others. However, what if you are not included in such reports? This is where many companies do a poor job because they will say, "It's our policy not to bad-mouth the competition. We stick to discussing our products."

Think about that for a minute. What the salesperson just said, in effect, is, "The only way we talk about our competitors is to bad-mouth them and we don't want to do that now, so you're on your own about comparing us to them."

Not a helpful message. It's much more productive to say: "It's our policy not to bad-mouth our competitors, but we can provide you with a factual analysis of how our product compares to several other leading providers." Then you do just that, on a webpage, with a download, or during a webinar.

Your factual helpfulness to your target accounts will stand in contrast to competitors who don't provide the information. That may have the effect of the prospect wondering, "Why don't those other companies provide it? What are they hiding?"

Damaging Admissions Increase Believability

It's worth taking a page from some of the most legendary copywriters, and include in your comparisons and descriptions what's known as a "damaging admission."

Here's the concept: just as prospects want to know who offers what they need, and how the vendors compare, they also want to know what are the weaknesses of each solution. People intuitively know what engineers have known for a very long time: "You can be fast. You can be high quality. Or you can be inexpensive—pick any two." In other words, nothing under the sun is simultaneously the highest quality, the least expensive, and the quickest to produce.

In B2B sales, it's no different. If I'm a logistics company, I can get your factory parts safely to the other side of the planet by tomorrow morning, but it is going to cost you.

Therefore, prospects consciously or unconsciously try to figure out the trade-offs for themselves, and the company that helps them to do it will stand out. If you don't describe how you're not perfect, then you force the prospect to search for the answer. If you do provide that information, you may have shortened that search for the answer.

Next, don't have one of those side-by-side comparison charts in which you have green checkmarks next to all features of your company, and the competition has a bunch of red X marks. Because you should know something about your target accounts, you can describe for whom your offerings are a good fit, and for whom they're not, and be honest about it. Add a few of those situations in your side-by-side comparison.

For example, one customer of Demandbase is a leader in software for running A/B tests and multivariate tests, among other things. It started out with a business model that had pricing options for the SMB market as well as at the enterprise level. After analyzing its customers and the marketplace, this company decided to focus its efforts on enterprise accounts. It didn't want to be all things to all companies.

Therefore, its "damaging admission" when comparing itself to competitors relates to price: if you're a relatively small business, and are just starting to do split testing, this company is probably not the best initial choice. That's factual and helpful, and it may allow the prospect to stop searching for the negatives.

> **Localytics on ABM**
>
> "We recognized that our marketing spend was inefficient and lead volume wasn't a valuable metric for us anymore. We knew there had to be a different way, a better way. That's when we had the idea to take an account-based approach. With our first pilot, we achieved a 36 percent account-to-meeting conversion rate."
>
> —*Vice President, Demand Generation*
> *Localytics*

Free Trials

Particularly with more-complicated B2B sales, an attractive option to test is offering a free trial. To maximize the results of a free trial, keep the following in mind:

B2B prospects are often more effort-sensitive than price-sensitive. For example, if you're offering a free trial of accounting software, the biggest objection to converting more visitors could be the perceived effort and risk of installing the new system, not to mention having to rip it out if they don't like it. This sensitivity could be far greater than any price objection.

Therefore, work closely with Sales to uncover such concerns, so you can potentially counteract them with testimonials about how easy it was to install and test the new system. Also consider having a video that walks people through the migration process, and shows how easy it is to revert to the previous system.

If your research gave you any clues about the product or service that the target account is currently using, then it is an opportunity to customize the page: explain how you have a written guide, checklist, demo, or video about how to migrate easily from that current product to yours.

Another way to counteract concerns about enterprise services is to have longer trials than the typical B2C offer of 30 days. Again, intelligence from Sales should indicate the minimum and also the comfortable amounts of time for any trial to occur. Having the offer of a trial extension can work well, and it would be a strong buying signal for visitors to take you up on the offer of contacting Sales to discuss a longer trial period.

One other point: if your free trial is fully featured, be sure to say so. If it comes with live installation support, make that be a prominent message. Whenever Sales identifies an objection and you have a good answer for it, consider adding that to your website and also possibly using that information in your content marketing.

Breaking through Breakage

If you haven't heard of the concept of breakage, it's useful to know. When something is offered but not used, that's breakage.

For example, let's say a company offered a subscription level for a service, where that level included a free 60-minute strategy session with one of their senior systems integrators. This can be a win/win for the company because of the perceived value of the strategy session, yet at the same time, many subscribers may not schedule one.

What does this have to do with converting? You need to manage breakage carefully, or in some instances it can become a barrier to conversions. For example, let's say you're Acme Services and you offer a 30-day free trial of your SaaS solution. It's valuable, considering the cost of the software. Your sales team is seeing a lot of target accounts that started the trial, and Sales can also detect that many of these people have not begun to use the trial software, nor have they generated any additional buying signals.

What may be happening is these opportunities are stuck in sequential thinking: "I'm interested in the software and want to do the trial, but just don't have the time. When I get around to the trial, then I'll be ready to decide about moving forward."

If Sales detects this sort of breakage or stalled motion in the trial, then a mere trial extension may just perpetuate the problem. It may be better to go for an intervention in the form of contacting the prospect and going for a live demo. "I know you're evaluating our trial software, but I wanted to offer a live demo, because there are a couple of features that you might not see in the trial." If you give a reason for the demo, it provides the prospect with a reason for now getting off the trial track and jumping over to the demo one.

This same kind of breakage can happen if people need to read through lots of materials and never get around to it, so they don't move forward with the purchase. When Sales and Marketing detect such behavior and put their heads together about how to resolve or even prevent it, more conversions are likely to progress to sales.

Best Practices for Webinar Conversions

We talked a little in Chapter 5 about how webinars are great tools for attracting leads. Now let's talk about how to maximize the effectiveness of webinars for conversions.

As we said, you're better off producing webinars in-house, so you have maximum control. Another reason for doing so is to take advantage of the three levels of ABM: one-to-one, one-to-few, and one-to-many. Webinars are excellent platforms for getting as broad or as targeted as you wish: you can produce one for a single account as the audience. And just as we talked in Chapter 5 about how you can often repurpose content with minor adjustments, you can create a warehouse of webinars that work for different accounts or segments with just minor alterations.

Because B2B sales involve very busy decision makers, it's important to take certain steps to make sure they register for the webinar, attend it, and actually stay to the end. Here are some points to keep in mind:

Quantify as much as possible what they will get out of the webinar. Too many webinars have titles that describe things without stating the benefit to the participant. Instead of a webinar about "Trends in CRMs for manufacturers," it should be "Five Research Findings about CRMs for manufacturers: May 2020 Update." It's quantified and freshness-dated.

Send a few emails ahead of the webinar, where you describe genuinely useful things they will learn on it. Decision makers' time is so valuable, and so many priorities appear every day, that you should continue to make the case for their attendance, even after they've registered. Otherwise the webinar will start to look like an easy time slot to free up.

Make sure your webinar technology vendor can give you analytics after the event. What you want to know is attendance in five-minute increments throughout the event. You need this to help you match the message that was being discussed when people left the webinar. This analysis will enable you to experiment with different content that may be more engaging and persuasive in those drop-off spots.

Also make sure your webinar provider tells you how long each registrant attended. As you know, the ABM mindset is about tuning the message to the target account recipient. Let's look at some examples:

- *Person A attended but left after five minutes.* Hypothesis: mismatch of topic to what Person A needed. Contact to confirm.
- *Person B registered but didn't attend.* Offer another time for the webinar.
- *Person C attended but left before your call to action.* Contact with offer for a quick summary of what they missed.
- *Person D stayed throughout, but did not convert.* Hypothesis: this person was engaged enough to consume the entire webinar, but there's an unanswered objection. Contact and ask if that is the case.

In addition to whatever personal follow-up you do, it's worth considering sending some emails after the event, especially to those who attended most of it but did not convert. A best practice is to have each email focus on one key objection that in your experience is raised by this point in the buying journey. By bringing up and then answering such objections, you may well get some of these attendees to the next level in the funnel.

One other point: consider sending a transcript to non-attendees or those who attended but left early. Some people much prefer to read at their own pace instead of listening at the pace of webinar presenters.

Lowering the CTA Bar

We'll discuss closing in the next chapter, but here we want to talk about an earlier decision—when a lead raises his or her hand and becomes an opportunity.

It doesn't take much to persuade visitors not to act right now, even if the action does not have major consequences. On the one hand, it's true that they're only being asked to get walked through a demo, attend a local event, or be on a webinar. Still, we can assume that we're only one of several possible contenders, and all these activities take time.

Decisions often feel like risks being taken, even if it's just the risk of the unknown: "If I leave my contact information, will I be mercilessly hounded?"

You can reduce that perceived risk in three ways:

1. **Explain what will happen after visitors raise their hands.** "The demo will take only 25 minutes" or "The webinar is 45 minutes and we'll have one of our senior engineers on the line afterward to answer questions."
2. **Restate any guarantees you have, right near the CTA.** Elsewhere you might discuss your guarantee, but don't assume that they read it. Make sure any guarantee is prominent near where you'll have them raise their hand.
3. **Reinforce the CTA with testimonials.** Again, you may have testimonials elsewhere, but it's near the CTA that the decision is being weighed to move to the next level. Provide social proof that companies like theirs have been satisfied with what you have to offer. It's especially effective if the testimonials list names and titles that are consistent with the job functions of your target accounts.

Another important factor in persuading people to act is the extent to which you deliver a cohesive message. If Marketing approaches target accounts with one set of messages, but Sales has its own spin on what's being said, prospects can easily become confused—and a confused mind does not buy. Therefore, take the time to ensure that your digital and offline channels are mirroring the conversations that Sales is having. This will help to speed up and support deals instead of slow them down or even derail them.

Case Study: Iron Mountain

Iron Mountain provides storage and information services to almost all of the Fortune 1000, and is a Fortune 1000 company itself.

They had three challenges with their B2B digital marketing activities:

1. How to reach target accounts effectively and attract them to their website
2. How to identify target accounts on the website and engage them with relevant content
3. How to increase conversion rates

Iron Mountain implemented ABM and addressed the challenge by first determining their target account list. Then they used display advertising to reach target accounts that had not visited Iron Mountain's website, and drive them there. Once the target accounts were on the site, they served specific messages for those target accounts.

At the same time that they were serving these targeted messages to certain accounts, Iron Mountain implemented A/B testing. This allowed them to measure engagement with targeted content for companies in specific verticals.

Iron Mountain then addressed the conversion challenge of getting visitors to fill out forms. They were able to reduce form fields from 16 to 12 but at the same time, ABM allowed Iron Mountain to append more information about those accounts. The result was fewer form fields, but more information.

Because Iron Mountain wanted to attract both SMBs and enterprise accounts, they looked hard at their analytics tools to determine whether these different segments interacted differently with the content on the site.

Iron Mountain then developed dashboards that allowed the inbound team to see what content attracted different accounts to the website, how it was engaging visitors, and what content most influenced conversions.

The Director of Internet Marketing at Iron Mountain, said, "Our first test, which targeted healthcare, showed a 120 percent lift in engagement." He went on to add: "If you display the right message to the right person at the right time, good things happen."

Some of the "good things" Iron Mountain experienced with ABM included:

- Finance and banking accounts showed an engagement lift of 115 percent
- Overall there was a 219 percent increase in conversions while capturing more and richer data
- They saw a 78 percent lift in page views and 36 percent lift in company engagement

The Director added: "Over the past year, our web lead volume has more than doubled."

Closing Accounts

We've succeeded in converting a number of accounts on your target list to opportunities. But at the end of the day, the work of the marketing team can only be considered "done" when a target account places an order with your company. Period.

That means the marketing organization must employ its entire bag of tricks to attract, engage, and convert those leads into opportunities. Then Marketing must support Sales in actually closing those accounts, and thus turning them into revenue.

As critical as the preceding steps are, we know that Marketers have traditionally not been focused in that way. It comes back to the graphic you saw earlier (see Figure 7.2).

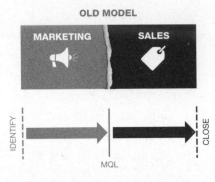

Figure 7.2   The old model of how Marketing and Sales worked "together"

As marketers, our job was done when we generated an MQL and threw it over the wall to Sales. By the same token, it really wasn't the problem of Sales to think about demand gen or lead gen. That was Marketing's job. This "silo" approach to the departments might be common to companies everywhere, but that doesn't make it any less frustrating to work within such a system.

In the more sophisticated and more effective world of ABM, things are different (see Figure 7.3).

Both teams have their separate roles to play, but both are involved throughout the process from identifying the target account list all the way to closing the accounts. Sales is involved in campaign conception and messaging, and Marketing is involved in getting that deal to contract signature.

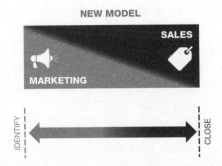

Figure 7.3   The new model of how we work together

As we've discussed, this is accomplished by communicating at a much more active level, aligning our incentives, setting goals together, and aligning our measurements.

For our sales colleagues to close as many deals as possible, they need as much relevant information on each account as possible. You can break this information into three groups:

1. **Background:** This is basic account information such as the size, locations, and industry vertical of the account. It also includes contact information such as title, phone number, and email address for key targets in the account.

2. **Activity:** Included in this group is data on website engagement, webinar and event attendance, and eBook downloads. As we mentioned earlier, any upward or downward swings can be powerful signals to Sales about an account's interest.

3. **Insights:** This third group has quickly become a critical tool to help win deals and close accounts. True insights differ from background and activity in that they are based on off-site behavior: what are accounts researching; what are they interested in; what keywords that are connected to your value proposition are they reading? Armed with this information, a great sales rep can have more relevant conversations with target accounts, and tailor his or her interactions with that account based on their interests.

World-class marketing teams think about the entire marketing *and* sales process, and arm their sales counterparts with the information and insights to help close their target accounts.

~ ~ ~

As final as it sounds to "close" an account, there's one other key function to perform, and that's to measure. In the next chapter, we cover this element of ABM that's so vitally important.

8

Measuring What Matters

What Effective Metrics Look Like for ABM

You may remember from earlier in this book that we said there were two central concepts to ABM and they should always be on your mind—accounts and revenue. It would not be incorrect to add the third concept of measurement.

Though it seems common sense that of course businesses know to measure regularly, in our experience the common sense does not always translate to common practice.

For example, certain types of brand awareness are extremely tough to measure. You may have spent six figures or more to have your logo appear on the wall of a sports arena, in view of television cameras. Good luck with tying that back to measurable results. That is not to say that all such money is wasted. Maybe there are intangible reasons for executives making those decisions. As long as they represent a small amount of the marketing budget, they may have a place.

We think that the vast majority of a marketing budget should be spent in ways where the results can be reliably measured.

Attribution

We know that the grass often seems greener where others live, but even so, we think the B2C marketers have it a little easier. We're referring to attribution, or the practice of trying to determine what action resulted in a conversion.

B2C sales can be complex if they involve, for example, the sale of a Gulfstream jet to the ultra-rich. But most consumer purchases are relatively short and transactional. A company runs an ad that's tagged to a specific phone number, so inbound calls can be tied to what generated them. The same is true with pay-per-click ads to a landing page that sells a product, or email blasts that generate sales based on a special offer.

With B2B sales, the journey tends to be much more complex, not only involving more time, but more decision makers. We think the actual path taken by B2B buyers looks more like what you see in Figure 8.1.

Between the length of the sales cycle and number of players involved, it's extremely difficult to determine which programs and touches matter the most. A traditional first touch/last touch attribution at the campaign level may not be the best way to measure your

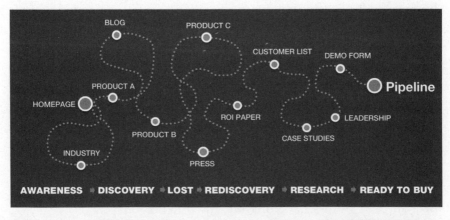

Figure 8.1   Attribution is much less clear in the B2B world

ABM strategy. We discuss some tools and software options in a later chapter, but want to remain true to our original statement in this book—that you should invest in ABM tools only after you've taken the steps to assemble a team and run a pilot.

Three Levels of Measurement

As you know, there is no shortage of yardsticks in business, but we find it useful to group effective measurements into three types: revenue performance; marketing performance; and campaign and web. Let's look in more detail at each.

At the highest level are revenue performance measurements. The C-Suite and board of directors want to know what they can take to the bank in terms of big-picture revenue, expenses, and profit. At this high level of reporting, ABM and non-ABM companies will look at similar outcomes: revenue by product line, by region, and so forth.

They also want to gauge the health of the business, and have as many leading indicators as they can in that regard. This is where companies active in ABM will differ somewhat from non-ABM ones.

Three crucial metrics at this level are close rates, average deal size, and funnel velocity. Where ABM companies differ is they have deeper insights into these numbers, after having carefully measured the effect of ABM on their business. As you know, the most effective way in our opinion to embed the ABM strategy into a company is to conduct a pilot. By taking baseline measurements and then running the pilot, it's possible to measure the results ABM has on these metrics versus traditional marketing.

After the pilot ends, these distinctions will persist, as ABM is rolled out to more territories, product lines, and accounts. Over time, the company will be in a position to understand more deeply what is affecting close rates, deal size, and funnel velocity, all of which in turn are leading indicators of revenue performance.

The next level involves all the marketing-performance metrics. These are department-level and team-level numbers for assessing how effective Marketing is at generating opportunities for Sales. It's what is on the dashboard for the CMO.

Which is better—having no leads or 100 of them? Our first instinct as marketers might be the wrong answer. If the hundred leads result in little or no business, then we're better off staying in bed, so to speak.

Therefore it's important to come up with metrics that can answer the following: Are your marketing results on track to meet the revenue-performance objectives? If so, great. If not, then what needs to change?

You'll be in a good position to answer what must change if you use the following marketing performance metrics:

Target account list engagement. This is a great leading indicator to see if your efforts are having an effect. Given that you are now focusing on a specific set of accounts, you should expect that this metric will go up. Let's say you have 100 accounts on your pilot target account list. If at the start of your pilot, 10 of them are engaging with you, maybe the goal for the pilot period could be to increase that number from 10 to perhaps 25. How you define engagement will be up to you, but it should be some meaningful way of demonstrating that there is interest in your offering from a particular account. For most organizations, it will be a combination of website visits, campaign engagement, and the number of unique contacts engaging within that account.

Pipeline. This is a good measure because it's a couple of steps removed from MQLs and it must be vetted by a salesperson who has committed to closing a certain percentage that are open. Not only do you want to measure overall pipeline compared to your quarterly goal, but also measure and report by week. That gives insights into good or bad trend lines and allows you to make adjustments along the way. If numbers are behind, you can have the conversation with Sales to see where the problem might lie: maybe Sales is currently understaffed in the SDR function; maybe Marketing has backed off a little too much on the volume of its programs; or maybe programs haven't been producing their historical levels of opportunities.

Percent of pipeline represented by target accounts. This important measurement helps you to understand how effective your ABM program is at filling that pipe with the right accounts. Problems detected here may indicate an issue with account selection, or a mismatch in messaging for those target accounts.

Number of target accounts on website. It's pretty well established that accounts that will buy from you will have visited your website in the course of doing research. If you begin to see a downward trend in this number, it's a good leading indicator about potential issues. Take our earlier list that was 100 accounts. Let's say that at your baseline period, you have 25 of the 100 visiting your website, but one quarter in, only 20 have visited. This should be a red flag that your attraction campaigns and activities aren't working. The task now becomes how to reverse that trend.

Conversion Rates. If these rates are going up, it's a solid leading indicator that your ABM strategy and tactics are hitting the mark. If your conversion from MQL to SAL goes up from 75 percent to 85 percent, that's a good indicator that your target account list is strong. If you also see your conversions going up at different stages along the pipeline, that's a sign that your programs are getting to the right people with the right message to keep these deals progressing toward closed–won business. If these metrics are not going up, you'll have some idea where to look to turn things around.

Influence. As we stated early in this chapter, attribution is a really tough metric to hang your hat on in B2B. Because there are so many touches that influence an account before and after it becomes an opportunity, you need to understand which programs as a whole (by channel or program type, versus specific campaign tactics) seem to move the needle when it comes to getting accounts into pipeline or from pipeline to close. Identifying where they are most useful in the process also helps the marketing team align its resources and touches where they are most needed to help close business.

Customer retention and upsell. It's sometimes the case that customers don't get the attention they once did. Keeping track of customers at all stages of the life cycle will help spot disturbing or gratifying trends. For example, an upward trend in customers renewing contracts after 24 months is worth noting and investigating, as is also the case if the trend is downward. The ultimate goal isn't just to renew what business you have, but also increase your share of wallet at that company. Watching these trends will point to where marketing programs are having an effect, and where they could possibly be improved.

Cost per opportunity. It's useful to compare cost-per-opportunity against number of opportunities. If your cost is decreasing and the number of opportunities is also decreasing, you have a mix of good and bad news. Time to investigate. The goal is to increase the number of opportunities while decreasing the cost per opportunity. This shows efficiency and effectiveness of reaching your target accounts and getting them into pipeline.

A Forrester study found that 77 percent of global B2B marketing decision makers surveyed said they lacked the ability to measure the results of ABM, and that it was a top concern.[1] Please notice how the preceding metrics not only measure the health of ABM in the organization, but also how well aligned these metrics are with what Sales cares about. None of these measures is volume for volume's sake. When mere volume is off the table and the focus across the organization is on the target account list, then that old volume focus is replaced by indicators of penetration and engagement of that all-important list.

Another way to align with the sales team is to make sure that reports are constructed in a way that is consistent with how Sales is structured. For example, some sales teams are organized around product lines, and others around account size, verticals, or geographic area. Reports should mirror that organization.

---

[1] https://go.forrester.com/blogs/6-metrics-that-matter-for-b2b-marketers-and-6-bonus-fun-facts/

The third level is the most granular—they are the campaign and web metrics. These are all the detailed measurements that roll up to the marketing-performance level, and those in turn roll up to revenue performance.

There can be dozens of these, relating to source of traffic and behavior on your site. They include page views, bounce rates, time on page, new versus returning visitor, and so on.

Where ABM differs from traditional measurements at this third, most granular level is we have a continuous focus on accounts and revenue. That means the campaign and web metrics only become interesting to the extent that they relate to the target account list.

Here's an example of that target-account focus: in Chapter 5, we described an experiment we performed. It showed that target accounts that engaged on our site after seeing account-based advertising converted into opportunities at a 60 percent higher rate. Focusing further advertising on these engaged target accounts results in more likely sales and directly rolls up to business outcomes.

A Global B2B Information Services Company on ABM: "As opposed to mass marketing, ABM works because it's so targeted and strategic. It keeps our sales channels focused on the end results because we have really long sales cycles."

—*Marketing Director, ABM*
Global B2B Information Services Company

In developing your campaign and web metrics, it's a good idea to start with the end in mind. No doubt you've already been tracking lots of elements at this level: What can you identify in regard to frustrations and what you would like to improve?

The next question is do you have metrics in place that cover each element of your marketing mix, so you can gauge its contribution to pipeline?

Signal versus Noise

One typical frustration in website analytics is with the amount of noise present. As mentioned earlier, engineers like to talk about the signal-versus-noise ratio, where what you want is the clearest signal and to eliminate everything else.

In the case of web metrics, the noise you should work to filter out is the traffic from accounts and individuals you can't or won't sell to: B2C companies, non-target accounts, vendors, your employees, job seekers, and your mom. Another nuisance is bot traffic, meaning automated software that visits your site and can sometimes be significant. This noise will throw off your metrics, analysis, and strategy if you don't filter it out.

Understand Key Segments

Once you have the noise to a minimum, you want to be able to segment the remaining visitors by the following:

- Prospects on your target account list
- Key industries
- Key geographies
- Current customers
- Former customers
- Lost prospects
- Key competitors

If you have not been segmenting in this way, you can look forward to an experience where it will feel like the lights just came on. You'll immediately see certain numbers jump out at you because they're much higher or lower than you thought they would be when you looked at the aggregate data.

Tools like Google Analytics can provide many insights if you're asking the right questions, after having filtered and segmented as we discussed earlier. However, because Google Analytics does not provide account-level metrics, you'll also eventually need an account-based analytics engine to provide that additional context.

When doing your analysis, you may see that one industry vertical—that you thought you had relatively low awareness with—is all over your website. Or the web page you thought was killing it as far as time on site was artificially inflated by non-target account traffic. Once you can look at these segments by comparing time periods, you'll get even more insights.

Then you want to find out what programs and campaigns are driving the audiences you care about to your site. The next analysis relates to behavior: which assets or pages receive disproportionately high or low attention? For the audiences you care about, which pages have unusually high exits from your site?

When you look at actions visitors take while on your site, how are those ranked? Where are the contrasts and anomalies when you drill down by geography, industry, prospect versus customer, and so on?

Sometimes companies will not take advantage of an analysis opportunity. They'll focus on how customers behave and not look so much at prospects. This can be a mistake. Think of it this way: your current sales and marketing systems converted certain accounts into customers. But the goal is also to determine what is going on with prospects that are just as qualified to become customers, but are not yet customers.

The analysis task then is to answer the question: "What is it about our qualified prospects that's different from our customers? Can we detect differences in their behavior, geography, industry, and other factors that it gives us a hypothesis to test?"

After you've done the work to set up all of what we discuss here—but before you take any action on these questions—you have something important to do, and we think by now you may know where we're going: you need to establish your baselines, as seen in Figure 8.2.

You need that stake in the ground or reliable starting point, against which you'll be able to measure results of actions you're taking after studying your analytics.

After you have your baselines, you can begin to ask a series of diagnostic questions that get at ways to improve. The first question is also the most fundamental: "Do I have enough web visitors of the type I want?"

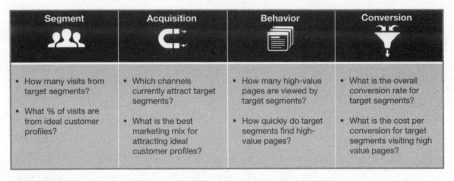

Segment	Acquisition	Behavior	Conversion
• How many visits from target segments? • What % of visits are from ideal customer profiles?	• Which channels currently attract target segments? • What is the best marketing mix for attracting ideal customer profiles?	• How many high-value pages are viewed by target segments? • How quickly do target segments find high-value pages?	• What is the overall conversion rate for target segments? • What is the cost per conversion for target segments visiting high value pages?

Figure 8.2   Be sure to establish your baselines

If the answer is no, then your focus should be on attracting them. If you do have enough visitors, then the next question is: "Do I have high engagement from the segments I care about that are on my site?"

This again brings you to a crossroads: if the answer is no, then you need to employ engagement techniques like analyzing and optimizing the content on your site.

Engagement can often be enhanced by taking the same content and serving it by way of different media. For example, some people like to read and others prefer to watch a video. By creating a short video of that very same content, you may increase engagement.

Problems with engagement could be due to other factors like site design that hinders engagement, or slow load times.

If you do have high engagement, then the next question is, "Do I have high conversions from my target accounts?" If no, then conversion optimization is needed. It could be that you have one form field that an unusually high percentage of people are leaving blank, or taking a long time to fill in, or abandoning the page altogether after they reach that field. In that case, you should consider whether you really need the field in the first place; or give it a better label (like what constitutes an acceptable password); or whether you can ask for that information later in the funnel.

It's not complicated, but instead a methodical, step-by-step approach to determining where the bottleneck to revenue is. Once you find a bottleneck and widen it with the appropriate methods, you move on to the next narrowing.

To summarize, you cannot go wrong by establishing the following baselines and regularly judging your success against them:

Short Term

- Conversion rates
- Target account list engagement
- Account penetration
- Influence

Medium Term

- Pipeline
- Cost per opportunity
- Opportunity rate (percent of opportunities coming from your target account list)

Long Term

- Close rates
- Average contract value
- Funnel velocity
- Revenue

Establishing Goals and Incentives

At some point—it could be before or after you establish benchmarks—it's time to determine goals.

Just as measurements need to be aligned, so do the goals, especially between Marketing, Sales, and Finance/Marketing-Ops teams. As we've mentioned several times, MQLs are an okay measure in the ABM world as long as they are more of a minor milestone at the campaign level to show early indications of performance. Even so, Sales doesn't want to hear about that metric. Sales will be interested to talk about the pipeline opportunities generated by Marketing.

Incentives get at the heart of the mindset shift with ABM because they tie a new way of thinking with a new way of getting paid. Marketing has traditionally been incentivized based on MQLs or some other number that we can completely control. As comforting and

seemingly logical as it is to be incentivized on things under your control, it has the effect of creating membranes or misalignment between
groups. It can foster the attitude of "Hey, we're making our numbers.
It's a shame if you're not."

In the ABM world, we're focused on making the same
fundamental numbers, even though there may be some relatively
minor differences. We will often underscore it with the graphic in
Figure 8.3, courtesy of Matt Heinz.[2]

What you can buy beers with (and might even get Sales to spring
for) are measures that are much closer to being converted into revenue, like pipeline. Of course, Marketing will never mirror the compensation of the sales team, but most teams will have quarterly variable
compensation incentives. When they are tied to these deeper funnel
metrics and even pipeline and corporate objectives, the result is that
both teams will be pulling in the same direction.

Account-Based Reporting Dashboard

In Chapter 3, we briefly mentioned dashboards to track ABM. Let's
look at the account-based reporting dashboard in more detail in
Figures 8.4, 8.5, and 8.6. These are usually together on one page but
for purposes of showing them in a book we have enlarged the sections.
This is an example of a dashboard used to track post-event success.

In Figure 8.4, we see primary metrics to understand what segments
were a part of this particular campaign. Then at the bottom we see that
it tracks the kind of opportunity generated, based on product lines.

In Figure 8.5, we see the breakdown of target accounts by SDR
and account executive. This is part of that sales enablement we talked
about earlier—making it easy for sales to identify the activities within
their accounts and act on it. Sure, they could look in the CRM campaign and sort the list by their name, but this is a far more visual way of
alerting them that their accounts are engaging.

In Figure 8.6, we see account distribution by customer success
manager (CSM). Note the bottom of Figure 8.5, where we also show

---

[2] https://www.heinzmarketing.com/

Figure 8.3   You can't buy a beer with an MQL

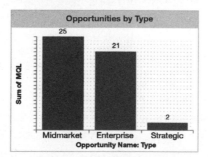

Figure 8.4   Part one of account–based reporting dashboard

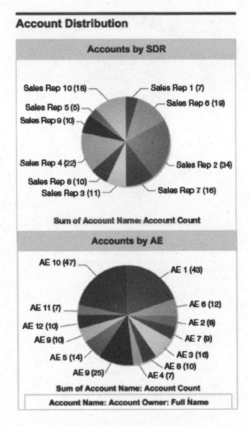

Figure 8.5   Part two of account-based reporting dashboard

a list of customer accounts. It's important to include accounts that have graduated from campaign to paying customer as a way of continuously keeping their value in mind.

Pipeline Dashboard

Because pipeline is such an important leading indicator of potential revenue, it deserves its own dashboard, as shown in Figures 8.7 and 8.8.

In Figure 8.7, we see the pipeline goal and achievement to date, which are metrics that give you visibility into how you're tracking toward your goals. It's also important to keep an eye on week-to-week trends: it's very important to understand the degree to which

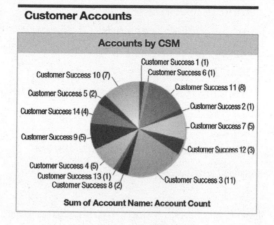

Figure 8.6   Part three of account-based reporting dashboard

programs are captivating segments at different points in the buyer's journey. The week-to-week numbers are also broken out by sales team in the same graphic. As we've discussed throughout this book, meaningful segmentation can highlight successes or problem areas that might be hidden when you look only at aggregate numbers.

In Figure 8.8, we see the distribution within pipe by different campaign types. Then at the bottom, we can see at a glance the backlog from open MQLs and SALs. As you focus on the higher quality leads that your target account list generates, the number of MQLs may decrease. Soon it should become clear that it's not a problem because your SALs and pipe should increase. Not only won't it be a problem, it will represent good news: it means your sales team will be spending less time on leads that never turn into buyers.

Reporting Your Results

Just as measurements need to be consistent at all levels and focused on accounts and revenue, so do the reports you'll generate.

At the CMO level, the following metrics should be continuously monitored:

- Target account list penetration
- Average unique contacts per engaged account
- Percent of target account list on the website
- Total pipeline generated
- Percent of pipeline coming from target account list
- Close rate
- Average deal size
- Closed–won revenue
- Cost per opportunity

Of course, the CMO will review much more granular reports as well, but these metrics deliver a lot of news at a glance.

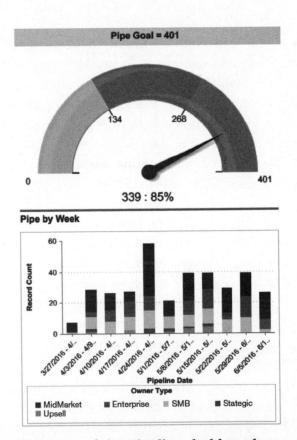

Figure 8.7   Part one of the pipeline dashboard

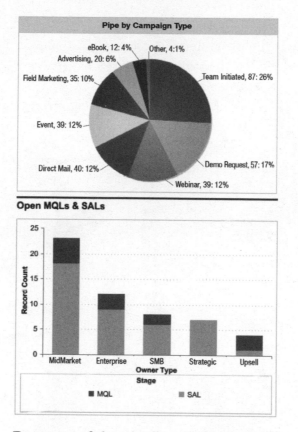

Figure 8.8   Part two of the pipeline dashboard

Then, at the department level, results get reported that are more specific to that area. For example, the head of Demand Gen would look at what is shown in Figure 8.9.

This person will want to see how each marketing channel is working, like content syndication, direct mail, and so on. There is also a graphic about each channel's contribution to both MQL and pipe goals.

Finally, the most granular level happens at the level of the program or channel owner, as seen in Figure 8.10.

The person who owns webinar campaigns wants to see not only the results of each webinar, but how they roll up to MQLs, SALs, pipe, and eventually closed–won status.

Figure 8.9   Reporting against forecast at the department level

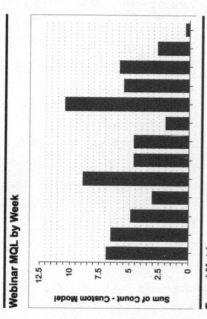

Figure 8.10 Reporting against forecast at the channel level

As with other reports we've discussed, the owner of this one can also get a sense of trends and use it as a leading indicator to take action if necessary to correct a trend.

Even though this report shows a substantial amount of detail, it summarizes other reports that are available to the webinar campaign owner as diagnostic tools.

For example, let's say one webinar has lower conversions than others. Using your webinar platform's analytics tools, it's possible to determine the average engagement of people watching that video. If the owner determines that there's a big drop-off at around 15 minutes into the webinar, that may be the cause of lower conversions—people are bailing out prematurely, so what was being discussed at Minute 15 such that people left in substantial numbers?

Then again, let's say the analytics indicate that there was no sudden drop-off and engagement was good throughout. That might indicate that there could be a problem with the offer at the end of the webinar or that the sales enablement was lacking.

This individual can also see where the webinars are really packing a punch: Is it pre-MQL or post-MQL? The numbers will make it clear whether webinars are helping to bring new accounts and contacts to the table for Sales to turn into pipeline opportunities.

Even at this highly granular level of analysis of a single event in a single channel, the overall concepts remain consistent around reviewing attraction, engagement, and conversions.

~ ~ ~

All the detail we've covered about measurements, goals, and reporting is focused on one purpose: to understand how your actions tie to the ultimate objectives of the business. If ABM did nothing else but focus an organization on accounts and revenue, it would be a highly successful methodology.

However, as you've seen in the chapters up until now, ABM is so much more. Now that we've covered the six pillars of ABM, from identifying accounts all the way through to measuring results, let's next discuss how to execute on ABM at a world-class level.

9

Scaling Your
ABM Efforts

How to Grow ABM Efforts Swiftly but Prudently

You've reached a major milestone: not only did you decide to try ABM, you also built a pilot. You then weathered all the issues and growing pains that are associated with any significant change, and you ran the pilot for enough time to generate data about its usefulness in your company with your type of customers. You also learned what ABM means to your organization, including the nuances that will make it work, given your size, complexity, corporate culture, and business model.

Congratulations, and we mean it: we know firsthand the journey you've been through, and just to travel it is worthy of a virtual high five.

You've had a chance to digest the pilot results with all the measurements we talked about in Chapter 8, so the big question is: Was it successful?

If the answer is no, then it's time to dig in and understand why not. Was it the way the target account list was created? If you reread

Chapter 4, you may have insights now that you didn't at the time. Now it may be clear that you bit off too much in regard to a pilot that was too large for your initial ABM capabilities. Then again you may have gone in the opposite direction and used too small of a group of accounts for you to be able to arrive at any meaningful conclusions.

Maybe your target account list was fine, but it was instead a matter of never finding that champion or two who would be patient as you occasionally had a setback or surprise.

We don't intend to list all the possible reasons, but suggest that you use your best judgment to go to the chapter where you think the problem may be, and reread the steps. You can be confident about the process we list because it's the result of not only our own experience with ABM but also our helping a great many companies to successfully travel down that path. If you're still not sure what happened, please contact us and we'd be happy to see if we can diagnose the issue.

Let's say, however, that you were able to conclude that the pilot was a success and you now have consensus for scaling ABM up from the pilot. The question is: How?

It's important to define what scaling really means. One way of scaling an ABM strategy is to expand your pilot to a full-ABM program across your organization. Scaling could also mean to do so across different segments from the ones you used in the pilot. Finally, it could mean scaling ABM across business units, regions, or across different product lines.

Six Questions to Ask Yourself

In a moment we will return to this question of how best to scale, but first let's assess where you are and where you should go from here, by considering several questions in a logical process.

1. Do you have positive results?

We covered this earlier, but it's important to say here that you shouldn't consider scaling until you understand what didn't work, and you take steps to fix it. Then you can test the new strategy and see if you get improved results before moving on to the next question. Otherwise, if you don't know why you did not have positive results but you try to scale, you'll likely repeat the same mistakes but on a larger scale.

2. Do you have repeatable processes?

Next, it's important to determine what processes you have in place and whether they are repeatable. Consider the programs you're currently running: Which of them are reaching your target accounts? Consider your segmentation strategy in the same way: Do you have a standard process in place for segmenting such that it can be followed by another business unit or region?

We suggested earlier that you do a post mortem if your pilot was not entirely successful, and determine the elements that may have caused that. But because we now assume your pilot was successful, in a sense we're asking you to do the opposite: think about the processes you followed to show positive results—are these written down somewhere? How complete are they? Are the procedures clear and easy to understand?

Continue to track and measure as you normally would, but begin to think about scaling as it relates to your metrics. At the outset of the pilot we recommended that you choose some segments or regions that would give you a reasonable chance at success, because you could concentrate your efforts in a few areas. The same is true now: ask yourself what would be logical extensions of the pilot, based on what worked well.

Conversely, if you had underperforming programs in the pilot, think about whether that program is fixable, or should it not be part of the scaling effort. It could be as simple as a bad vendor or partner that couldn't satisfy your ABM needs for a particular program. Most likely you can find a better one out there to work with you. Or maybe it was a lack of ABM knowledge by some other participants in your pilot. Fortunately, lots of materials exist to help get the rest of your team up to speed. One option is to send them to the Demandbase online certification so they get a solid understanding of the building blocks of a successful ABM strategy.

3. Do you have organizational buy-in?

A large part of a successful buy-in process is knowing how your organization is structured and where to expect resistance. It's of course no surprise to you that not everyone will be happy to embrace ABM. In fact, you probably encountered that situation when you were setting up the pilot. It's realistic to expect some holdouts, so think ahead of time about why they might be skeptical, even after the pilot results became known.

You should approach the conversations with confidence by showcasing your solid ABM results to date. It may be that this confidence and positive attitude will set the tone for ABM in a way that softens or eliminates much of what the naysayers have to say. If you do get some push-back, then it's okay to say that you don't have all the answers and of course can't know how ABM will work in every segment, every territory, and so on, but that it's worth a try, given the documented success so far.

Be sure to highlight the success stories, and have it come from multiple people. Let the reps who are seeing success in working the pilot accounts tell their colleagues in their own words why this "ABM stuff" is legit. This can be a very effective strategy because sales reps have competitiveness built into their DNA and won't want to miss the boat on something that's working well for others.

4. Do you know where to scale?

One of the most important considerations when scaling is identifying where it is that you actually will be most successful at scaling, given the realities of your organization. As always, consider your business objectives: if you're well aligned with corporate objectives, then executive sponsorship will be easier to obtain. You may even get more budget for ABM if the goals of your strategy are clearly laid out.

Now consider the decision whether to expand your ABM strategy to a new region or business unit: Do you have a clear playbook that is detailed enough that it can be applied to a specific region or business unit? People are notorious for thinking "my situation is different" even when it's fundamentally not. Therefore if your playbook does not mesh well with another region or business unit, expect that sort of pushback. Think about what it would take to adapt the playbook so it would fit well; maybe just changing some of the language in places would help it fit better. Finally, ask yourself: "Have I aligned with the ABM champions in my organization?"

It may save a lot of effort to work as much as possible during the early scaling with willing participants who are committed to working through issues because they can now see the value of ABM. If you are considering expanding ABM into a certain area like a division, think about who in that division has bought in and would be positive and productive to work with in scaling the ABM strategy there. If you can't think of anyone, that may make it difficult to source funding and resources for ABM there, and it may be an indication that this particular division is just not ready for ABM at the moment.

You obviously read books, or we wouldn't be having this discussion. We can recommend an excellent book to you called *Crossing the Chasm* by Geoffrey Moore.* It's about the groups of people you will encounter when you attempt to roll out a new technology. Moore says they break down on a bell curve as follows:

- **Innovators.** This tiny group actively seeks the next thing, and they need zero persuasion.
- **Early Adopters.** People in this medium-size group may not be seeking something new, but are willing to try it early on, because they trust their intuition.
- **Early Majority.** This is a large group of people who are open-minded but practical. They want to see some proof and that the bugs have been worked out before they jump in.
- **Late Majority.** This is also a large group. They want the same proof that the Early Majority wants, but they differ in

(continued)

---

* G. A. Moore, *Crossing the Chasm: Marketing and Selling Disruptive Products to Mainstream Customers* (New York: HarperBusiness, 2014) one respect: they want lots of support for them to sign up, so they wait for the technology to have a large, established support ecosystem.

- **Laggards.** This medium-size group will adopt something only when there is no other choice and the new technology is no longer new, but embedded in daily life.

When you're planning to scale to a particular region or division, we suggest that you discreetly think about where people in that area fall among these five types. You can tilt the odds of success in your favor by seeking people from the first three types. Then you'll have scaled enough that the Late Majority folks should be ready to come on board. Never mind about the Laggards.

5. Do you know how it will affect budgets?

Your ABM strategy may have worked well for the pilot or for one division, but when you're creating the scaling playbook, consider your budget and marketing mix: How might that need to be adjusted for a different business unit or region? You know, of course, that budgets aren't just going to balloon ahead of demand no matter how successful the pilot was. You'll need to show positive results first, but it will be difficult for others to accept if you have not planned for cost measurement. ROI reporting is crucial here: you must be able to show the cost efficiencies you will be creating by scaling ABM to a new division. To help frame your budgeting guidance, review Chapter 4 to understand where some of those trade-offs between cost, volume, and precision come into play.

6. Do you know how it will affect your marketing team?

A common misconception with ABM is that because the word "Marketing" is in the name, people think the marketing team will all understand it and be aligned. That is frequently not the case. Marketing departments have a variety of different functions, management structures, and even different goals. Therefore, ABM goals need to be set across the entire marketing organization. Each functional area of Marketing needs to be prepared for what ABM can bring, but each one also needs to understand what it will take to make ABM successful.

Just as we recommended that you privately assess where people are in regard to Innovators versus Early Majority and so forth, you need to do a similar assessment about the skills across the organization: Is the entire team prepped and skilled to focus on target accounts and to connect marketing activity to revenue? Do you anticipate the team mix changing, and if so, is there a plan for communicating about this upcoming change and implementing it? As you scale ABM, is everyone involved aware of each other's roles, responsibilities, and time lines? These are a lot of considerations, but they all must be dealt with in order to ensure that your entire marketing team is ready for this change.

Your ABM Playbook Is Crucial

If you made it through all six of these main questions, you are now in an excellent position to create your ABM scaling playbook. And you do need a playbook: it's one thing for people to agree to a pilot. After all, even the Laggards might shrug and not put up opposition because it's not their area that's doing the pilot, and besides, they're sure it will be a failure.

Now that you have a successful pilot to point to, that starts to change the dynamic. "You mean this ABM thing that they were working on—you now want *us* to consider being part of it?" Even if you have the relative luxury of being able to scale to areas where you have some Early Adopters, still it's change management that we're talking about here. The more detailed your playbook is, the smoother will be the process of moving one group after another to the mindset and system that is ABM.

Even though we're discussing how to scale from your successful pilot, we're guessing that you're reading this book through before even starting that pilot. Smart move. Another smart move will be for you and the pilot team to become obsessive in a good way: as you go through the pilot process, document everything. After you go through a challenging project like a pilot, it's easy to forget the granular issues and decisions you made on daily basis. Your playbook will be a long way toward becoming comprehensive if you just keep detailed notes as you go.

Don't worry about presentation as you do the documenting. There will be time later to make things pretty and organized. Just get the details down. Your playbook will eventually have the kind of detail that would make NASA proud, and it will make your persuasion job easier.

Let's assume that you're done with the documenting, and then the organization and presentation of the playbook. It should clearly show how to expand your ABM strategy into different types of new areas of the business—a new territory, different business unit, and so on. It should also define the process and provide people in leadership, Marketing, Sales, and Operations with everything they need to repeat the successes of the ABM pilot.

Let's now look at how to enable those four areas in order for the ABM scaling effort to be successful.

Enabling the ABM Leadership Team

Transparency and communication will be the key to getting full support from your leadership. Think about the reports you plan to share across the scaled-up ABM team: Will the leaders of the business units have access to the same reports? They'll need those reports before they give their buy-in and see how the strategy is unfolding.

Some of them may need to see the data again on how the target accounts performed in the pilot versus the baseline. Just as you needed to establish those baselines before launching the pilot, you'll need to do the same thing now, before launching ABM in another area. You should also be prepared to discuss how ABM affected the pilot group's marketing mix, so the leaders know more about what to expect as they adopt ABM elsewhere.

Expect to meet on a regular basis to discuss the many topics that make up the process of launching ABM in a new area. Set expectations ahead of time about the frequency of meetings and which stakeholders need to be at each one. Try to get calendar time blocked off for weeks to come or even longer, because otherwise we both know what will happen: it will be a pain to compare calendars after every meeting, and soon there will be attendance issues or postponed meetings. These don't have to be long, drawn-out meetings. They need to be regular, though, with the necessary people in the room or on the phone.

You might meet to review list quality once per quarter, but you should review performance metrics much more frequently, depending on the length of your sales cycles. If you have three-to-six-month cycles, then meeting weekly is a good idea. If the cycles are only one or two months long, you may need to meet a few times each week to ensure that performance is tracking, and to handle any issues before they get away from you.

Enabling Marketing

The entire Marketing team should be preparing for ABM success and all that comes with it, now that they'll be working on it actively—instead of just the folks who were part of the pilot.

Now is the time to show how the marketing mix will change with an ABM focus versus the previous way of doing business. Show the adjustments you made initially in the pilot, and any subsequent tweaks and the reasons behind them. This will allow them to plan ahead and make educated decisions to help reach success faster.

Make sure the format of your reports is consistent across all marketing programs so the sales team doesn't get confused and miss key opportunities to engage in a sales conversation. Making the change from old way to ABM way is a large enough cognitive load. Don't add to it by making people decode different report parameters when they could have been standardized. A consistent report can build confidence as they begin to look at different campaigns and their performance.

Create a performance dashboard that brings together the different reports and gives everyone easy access to performance data with a couple of clicks. Configure and update these dashboards based on how you organized your strategy: by team, campaign, vertical, product, time period, and so on. The goal is to have no ambiguity for marketers who will now be adopting a new way to evaluate their performance. Just as with Sales, make sure you keep Marketing focused on reaching the target accounts, and not on debating whether ABM is right for them. It's already been piloted and was successful. It's now being rolled out so other areas can enjoy the same success, and our focus is on doing what's necessary to maximize that result.

You'll probably have to emphasize more than once that marketers must be tied to the same funnel metrics that are being used to evaluate the effectiveness of the ABM strategy in this new scaled-up project.

The marketing people must also know how they will be compensated in an ABM world in order to eliminate confusion and rumors and keep them focused on the metrics that will drive the desired results.

Use the results of your pilot to show them how the ABM strategy has affected performance and how they can approach forecasting the performance in their own area. If you've seen dramatic increases in metrics like close rates, average contract value, and opportunity generation, share those numbers and encourage them to establish their own benchmarks. You might even show them a spreadsheet with your results overlaid on their benchmarks to give them a sense of what will happen when they do indeed implement the full ABM strategy.

When it comes to the campaigns and segments to be focused on, everyone on the marketing team needs to understand the business objectives for each campaign. Then align them with your segmentation strategy: Which segments are the highest performing ones? Which are in highest demand? The dashboard should also indicate which campaigns are currently running and which are about to launch as well as which audience segment is involved in each.

This needs to be common knowledge among everyone on the marketing team, and regularly updated as well. This will prevent some segments from being over-marketed to, resulting in message fatigue. If specific segments are kept in mind within the target account list, then they should only receive messages that are appropriate and timely.

Make sure to validate this by looking at both the account level and at the individuals within those accounts. For example, you probably should send a different message to contacts that are engaged versus those that aren't. Your campaign communication strategy should consider audiences at this level of detail.

Engaging and Enabling Sales

No ABM strategy can succeed without the support of your sales team, no matter how effective you were at identifying your target account list, or how creative the campaign design was.

Make sure you vet new programs with your sales team. Do they think a particular program will be effective? Why or why not? They don't think certain messaging will resonate? That's fine. they should help you come up with messaging that is closer to what they're hearing out in the field. Engaging Sales upfront does two things: it will improve your overall campaign messaging and execution and it will ensure more success due to Sales buy-in.

"Sales enablement" has traditionally been the job of the product marketing team. It involved creating pitch decks, FAQs, competitive analyses, and other materials that were delivered to the sales team.

In an ABM world, everyone needs to wear a sales-enablement hat at times, because that enablement must dive deeper into details than it did previously. Sales needs to just not have the collateral materials, but also understand the contexts: if you recently built a campaign, then your sales-enablement hat means that you'll now document that context. You'll explain why you decided to create this campaign; what is the campaign about; what is the expected next action by Sales; and what are some good call scripts and email templates. If those scripts or templates are unusual in any way, then why are they worded the way they are; what is a good CTA for following up, and so forth.

If you want Sales to be active participants in your programs, then you must provide them with this granular level of detail and all the assets they'll need to fulfill your requests. You'll also need to provide goals and metrics as they relate to your shared target account list.

When Sales Enablement Doesn't Happen

At a recent ABM conference, Jessica was catching up with another attendee whom we'll call Jorge. He said that he'd recently spent $50,000 on a direct-mail campaign that resulted in literally zero revenue. He added that it was because the sales team had not bought into the mailing list for this campaign on the front end, and he hadn't taken the time to enable Sales on the back end.

Jorge said that he could now see that his marketing unit thought, in effect, "We're going to do ABM with this mailing and Sales is going to love it." But Sales never vetted that list, so they weren't invested in it. The leads just showed up in the CRM and they had no idea what to do with them.

The reaction from Sales was, "That's great that you got all these names from a list that *you* put together—but they're not the names that *we* care about."

It's vital that you provide support in their language and on their terms. For example, handing over a massive database to Sales and saying: "Everything you need to know about the next campaign is all in here" will do nothing but frustrate them.

At Demandbase, we've developed over time what we call the Marketing Center. It's an intranet in which we have every asset and event organized in a way that Sales wants to see it—we know that because we asked. You can see the main page in Figure 9.1.

Each of these menu items has submenus under it in great detail. So, for example, a sales rep might think, "Oh, I know there's this dinner coming up. I need an email template for it." In the old days, the rep would have contacted us to ask for it. We'd say, "We sent that to you last April," to which the rep says: "Yeah well I can't find it. Could you send it again?" This lose/lose situation has been replaced by a win/win one: Sales has at its fingertips all the information about every campaign that's currently in flight whether it's a digital one or in-person.

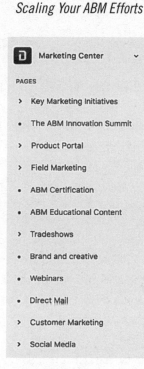

Figure 9.1   Our Marketing Center has everything Sales needs to work with us on campaigns

By the way, early in the design of the Marketing Center, someone in Marketing thought it should be organized by functions within Marketing. After all, it's called the Marketing Center. That would have meant, for example, that webinars could be found by going into "Digital Marketing" and then they would be listed in there. By looking through an ABM lens—which meant tight alignment with Sales—it soon was obvious that such an organization was not how Sales looked at things. They'd think, "Where is that webinar?" It's therefore organized under "Webinars." It's a small distinction but we've found that they add up over time. This type of sales enablement has made a big difference for us.

Now, when we are about to add campaign materials to the Marketing Center, we run through a list of questions to make sure we've covered all of the bases:

- What's the goal of the campaign?
- Which target accounts are included in the campaign?

- What activities can Sales expect from Marketing? This includes links to all the materials.
- A calendar with all campaign-related dates
- Links to any relevant web pages
- What are the expectations of the sales team?
- What is the core messaging that they can leverage, either at the pre-campaign stage, or at the post-campaign follow up? In other words, actions they can take that will be consistent with the campaign messaging, but that are not part of the campaign itself.

If it's an event:
- What is the main Call to Action after the event?
- Locations of events, and photos of the venues
- Who will be presenting and what is the agenda?
- Promo codes for Sales to use
- Revenue or Pipeline in the Room Goal
- Goal for the event in regard to SQL/SAL/Pipe

We've found that this simple checklist not only makes it faster to assemble the complete package for Sales, but it also reduces the back-and-forth that happens along the lines of: "Hey, what is the address of the venue?" and then "Oh sorry, I'll shoot that over to you."

This sales-enablement support does not stop with marketing materials: Sales also needs reporting and dashboard support to make sure they're tracking toward success. That involves campaign, monthly, and quarterly performance and pipeline dashboards along with campaign prioritization recommendations from Marketing. We covered this in Chapter 8 when we discussed campaign dashboards.

It comes down to continuously asking yourself: "Does Sales have everything they need to fulfill the requests from Marketing? What else can Marketing do to help Sales, given that our overall goals are the same?" You may be asking them to drive a certain number of registrations, but if they don't fully understand the campaign, the goals, and the ask, it will be nearly impossible for them to meet your expectations. The job of Sales is difficult enough without making it even harder when goals and details are unclear, or campaign materials are scattered.

Enabling Operations

Up until now we've mainly talked about how vital it is to the success of an ABM strategy for Sales and Marketing to work much more closely than is typically the case. Another highly important partner is Operations, which acts like guardrails, keeping everyone moving in the right direction. Marketing Ops helps keep Marketing and Sales continually focused on the main goals of ABM through a suite of reports and dashboards.

They will also play a large role in building and maintaining the target account list by continuously bringing data to the table to help inform the list. They coordinate any list edits by both Marketing and Sales, and own the process for updating that list. Finally, Marketing Ops builds in the triggers in your technology to help track the list, starting with making it simple to identify and pull reports out of your CRM to evaluate and work with the list.

As if that's not enough, Marketing Ops also owns the tech stack. It is their responsibility to customize existing technology so it can properly execute your ABM strategy and evaluate and implement new technology to help you meet your goals. Therefore, make sure you have Marketing Ops at the table during all discussions about monitoring and reporting during the scale-up.

Now that you're scaling, and have some new internal areas to work with like an additional business unit or territory, consider how the funnel and overall model should be adjusted. Ask: "What do we need this quarter, next quarter, and one year from now, in order to grow?" Of course, you'll be monitoring close rates, average contract value and increases in pipeline as you did before. Another measurement could be bookings goals by period.

With the scaled-up teams—or their representatives—in the room, now is the time to determine how different teams have been measuring performance. Of course, by this point, they should not be focused on lead quantity and other similar old measurements; but even so, expect some lively discussions as people become accustomed to the ABM way of measurement, and also as the team makes adjustments that reflect the reality of the scaled effort. For example, if a different business unit is now part of the effort, there may be changes in the marketing mix with some channels added that were not part of the pilot. At the end of this realignment process, there needs to be consensus about what constitutes "success."

Five Ways to Find the Budget for ABM

Budgets can be a bit like oceangoing vessels: they are sometimes large, and once they get going, it's difficult to change their direction and momentum. Early in this book when we discussed how to find the budget for your ABM pilot, we said that a proven approach was to scrounge some resources, so to speak: find ways to avoid a formal approval process for the relatively small pilot, and try to draft off other initiatives as best you can.

Now that you're out of the pilot and are scaling the effort, budget becomes a more complex issue: on the one hand, you have the objective pilot measurements to point to, which will be persuasive. On the other hand, it may still be challenging to justify a significant spend if there hasn't been an extensive history of ROI—and if the areas you're scaling into have no history with ABM. They may also have a longer sales cycle than what you encountered in the pilot, and that only adds to the challenge.

Fortunately, we've seen ABM implemented in a great many organizations, including our own, and can suggest five ways to make the budget process go as smoothly as is realistic.

1. Have a top-down directive in place

This of course is not always the case, but sometimes it's possible to obtain an ABM-specific budget directive relatively early. This means you'll not only have high-level buy-in to implement ABM, but you have dedicated funds as well. After all, ABM is not a peripheral activity that takes away from the main business of the company—it's central to accelerating that business. At any rate, if you have such a directive early on, consider yourself fortunate.

Even with such support, you need to think hard about the processes and tools you have in place to support ABM. Is your CRM set up to mesh well with the level of detail that ABM requires? What about your marketing automation system? Be thorough in your review of the reports and dashboards you will need in order to track toward your goals so you can prove the ROI of this spend six to 12 months from now.

2. Make use of an innovation budget

Although marketing budgets may be larger than in Sales, a lot of that budget has traditionally gone toward demand-gen activities. As a result, most marketers have only a little latitude in their budgets, and it's typically used to test new methods or approaches to marketing. Of course, the number varies. What we've seen internally and among our customers is that the budget available for R&D, so to speak, is somewhere around 10 percent of the overall marketing budget.

One issue relates to some of the downstream metrics we've discussed, like average contract value, close rates, and funnel velocity. They can be excellent indicators of success, but they take time to accumulate significant numbers of data points. It's therefore important that you have some upstream metrics that let you know sooner whether you're on the right path.

3. Partner with other teams

Some marketers have been successful at approaching other units like Sales and asking for budget assistance. Before ABM, it would be pretty hard to imagine this sort of thing being successful, but by this point—after a successful pilot and now the hopes of even more success—such a request has a better chance of getting approved. It's especially true given the shared focus on accounts and revenue that you've established.

Sales departments always have some budget to support their technology needs like CRM or sales-enablement tools. It's worth making the case that the tools we eventually need to invest in for ABM will offer a variety of insights for Sales to leverage. For example, they'll get insights into anonymous buyer activity, interest by prospects in particular products, and even visibility into stalled deals. Of course, if Marketing does end up getting budget support from Sales, it's important to work hard to show the win/win outcome of this investment.

4. Roll it up under other initiatives

This works during a pilot but it can also account for at least some budget during a scale-up. For example, if you are undergoing a website redesign, it would be natural to make sure that the project benefits from ABM thinking: you want to check that the redesign team is using account-level data to inform the design. They should also consider adding a website-personalization tool to increase results like time on site, pages visited, number of sessions, form conversions, or downloads of specific pieces of content by particular accounts or segments.

What you want to make sure you do is ultimately be able to compare the metrics of these personalization efforts to the regular, nonpersonalized site messaging. Not only will that justify the spend, it may make the case for even more budget for expanded activities. It also, of course, will make it that much easier to justify the budget in other business units or territories when you scale up again down the road.

Marketing automation is also a typically hefty expense for marketers. If you need to reconfigure your MAS to be more account-centric or make some other ABM enhancement, there are tools that can help you accomplish this. The line item for MAS could therefore be another place where you can take care of some necessary budget for the ABM effort.

Remember that you may be able to phase your request, in the sense that you start with one aspect or segment and then scale from there once you have the data on its performance.

5. Shift or reallocate budgets from existing programs

As we discussed in Chapter 5, you'll definitely revamp your marketing mix after looking at channels with your new focus on the target account list. By the same token, many marketers take the approach of finding budget by reallocating funds with ABM in mind. Where this may not have been as possible during the relatively small pilot, now that the scale-up is happening, there may be more justification for shifting line items, because the scale is large enough now to make those budget savings meaningful.

The key to this approach is to accurately identify what's working and what is not. To do this, first get a list together of your current budget items. Sort the list by spend and look hard at the likelihood of each line item to reach your target accounts. For those items with less significant returns or likely engagements with your target accounts, you may be able to do some provisional reallocation to other, ABM-focused programs. We say "provisional" because it may take some of the pressure off the decision if you're approaching the decision as a test to see if the reallocation makes sense, and not as a budget decision cast in stone for all time.

Orchestration

This term is something of a buzzword in Marketing, but unlike some buzzwords that may have a short shelf life, the concept of orchestration is pretty fundamental to making ABM work in your organization. Even though it's not unique to the action of scaling your ABM strategy, we bring orchestration up here because without having it in place, you'll find any scaling efforts to be much more difficult than they need to be.

It's called orchestration but maybe it should be called choreography, because—just like a dance performance—each element needs to be continuously positioned with respect to every other element. It's about tightly tracking and coordinating activities across channels and across teams.

Sometimes the best way to describe something is to give an example of when it was not in place. Early in Jessica's career, she was working at a company that was in the teleconferencing industry. The company was a leader in on-premise solutions but competitors were starting to take market share by offering cloud-based solutions.

Jessica's company developed a strong SasS-based solution, which would take back some of that market share. They put together a campaign, consisting of web pages, emails, advertising—the works.

They hit "Go" on the campaign, and the first message in the campaign was sent to everyone in the database.

That high five glow lasted approximately five minutes, until the first phone call came in. It was the first of many from every sales rep who said—we'll sanitize this—"What did you just do? I just heard from my account, who already had our contract in hand and was ready to sign. Now my deal is stalled for a number of months because they have to evaluate whether they want to do an on-premise or SaaS-based solution! Oh, and now they're going to consider all the other SaaS competitors!"

Now that's lack of orchestration. Sure, Sales knew about the product, and they knew that we were going to run a launch campaign. But nobody brought up, "Hey, what should we do about accounts that are already in a sales cycle with us?"

Orchestration is making sure that you're in lockstep with your sales team. It's continually seeing to it that you are not putting messages out to the marketplace in general or a segment of your target account list if that message differs from what your sales team is delivering. Is it work to be that tightly coordinated between many people who are scattered everywhere? Yes. But it's more work, more painful, and less profitable to pick up the pieces when orchestration doesn't take place.

The Flip Side—Sales and the CRM

What comes around, goes around: just as Marketing must take the time and effort to stay in lockstep with Sales about messaging, Sales in turn must up its game as well in this new ABM world. We're referring to how the CRM is used—or in this case, not used enough.

CRM systems are only as good as the information they contain, and the problem historically has been that sales reps are spotty at best in updating the CRM to reflect the current status of accounts. Their thinking is, "Look, I make it my business to know about my accounts but it's tough enough to stay on top of my accounts. I don't have the time for paperwork just so someone back in the office can feel like the records are complete. Do you want me out writing reports or closing deals?"

That's a nonstarter approach in the ABM world. ABM is a team sport and can only be a team sport. In our experience, sales leadership has always tried to get their reps to update the CRM, with mixed success. ABM ups the ante so that leadership can say, "Hey, not only do I need you to update the CRM so we can report on where we are month to date, quarter to date, and so on, but Marketing really needs it now, too. If it's updated, that will allow them to run marketing programs in tandem to where you are in the sales cycle. That's directly going to help you close more deals."

~ ~ ~

You're out of the pilot and have your ABM processes set up and documented. With your playbook in hand for scaling it, you'll be picking up speed pretty quickly. Now it's time to discuss the options you have available for adding technology to your ABM effort in ways that can potentially make your work easier while enhancing profits.

10

Enhancing ABM with Technology

How to Pick the Right Technology to Maximize the Effectiveness of Your ABM Strategy

By this point we hope we've thoroughly made our case that you cannot buy your way into an ABM strategy. If you have technology but don't have a strategy in place, then you won't have clearly defined objectives or use cases for your technology, and you won't be able to prove the ROI for it.

At the same time, we recognize that when you see that this chapter is about adding technology to your ABM effort, a little voice inside is saying: "Not more technology! We're already drowning in what we have! We're not even using what we have effectively, never mind adding to it."

In a sense, we agree with your little voice because of two numbers: 17 and 6,800. The average tech stack in a B2B company includes

17 applications,[1] and more than 6,800 marketing technologies are out there.[2] It's quick to watch demos and write checks, but it's slow and difficult to do a methodical job of matching the needs of your business with the right technology, given the thousands of options.

To make matters more interesting, it's not like you can decide to wipe the slate clean with your existing tech stack; you need to make any additions fit in as seamlessly as possible with what you have, and it all needs to happen while staying open for business.

Therefore here is the most fundamental question: Is your ABM strategy ready for additional technology?

Identify Current Gaps

The first thing to evaluate is how technology worked—or did not work so well—during your pilot. For example, you built your target account list, but if you found it extremely painful to pull together the data sources in the account selection process, make a note of that pain point.

What else stands out as a really difficult task that surely could have benefitted from technology? For example, the important job of aligning measurements between Sales and Marketing is best done by people; but what about something like reporting: Was it a huge pain to go to multiple systems and try to collect data for the same period on the same accounts? That's another gap to make a note of in addition to any others you can think of, like difficulty with attribution, and so on.

This is an important step because, of course, budgets are limited for additional technology. By identifying the gaps or difficulties in the pilot, you're going to lay the groundwork that enables you to do three things:

---

[1] http://go.radius.com/rs/radius/images/The-Guide-to-the-Marketing-Technology-Landscape.pdf

[2] https://chiefmartec.com/2018/04/marketing-technology-landscape-supergraphic-2018/

1. It will help you to make the business case for getting technology to address those gaps
2. Knowing the gaps will also go a long way toward setting the objectives for additional technology
3. Because you did these functions the hard way in the pilot, now you'll be in a better position to calculate an ROI for the technology after you deploy it

Now that you've identified the main gaps, it's time to make sense of those 6,800 marketing technologies out there regarding how to review them while maintaining your sanity.

The ABM Tech Stack

Because we think about ABM all the time at Demandbase, we've been able to roll up our sleeves and organize all those offerings into what we consider to be a logical classification system, as you can see in Figure 10.1.

Let's now look at the five major areas of the tech stack in terms of what they contain and who benefits from them.

Infrastructure Technologies

How Do You Track and Execute Your ABM Strategy?

Within this family of tools, you have the following:

- Customer relationship management (CRM)
- Marketing automation systems (MAS)
- Data management platforms (DMP)
- Content management systems (CMS)
- Tag management
- Live chat

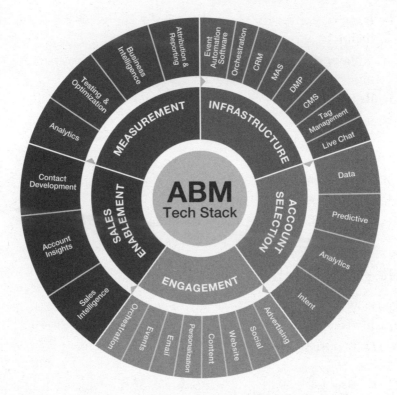

Figure 10.1   How to think about the ABM tech stack

Of course, the chances are excellent that you already have one or more of these technologies in place in your organization. Some of them, like a CRM and MAS are central to any B2B business—whether it's engaged in ABM or not. Other ones, like tag managers, are more specialized.

It makes no sense for us to even attempt to name names, in regard to which companies offer which solutions because that list changes daily. It also is not possible for us to get specific in this book about whether you truly need, for example, a tag manager or an orchestration technology. You may already have some of the technologies in place, and may not be feeling any pain from the absence of some of them in your stack.

ROLES AFFECTED:

Marketing Operations	Sales Operations	Demand Generation Manager	Sales/SDRs
Events Manager	Field Marketing	Website Manager	Content Manager
Social Media Manager	Creative/ Designer	In-House Ad Buyer	Sales Enablement

Figure 10.2   Get these people in a room to determine infrastructure tech needs

That's why it's important to have identified your gaps first, so you can then have something of a specific shopping list for technologies to close those gaps. In general, infrastructure technologies help you with the following:

- Lead routing and prioritization
- Reporting on accounts
- Acting on accounts
- Cleaning bad data

When thinking whether it's time to add to this part of your tech stack, it will be crucial for you to get together with the people who are most affected by them. You can then refine your collective gaps list of what you hope the technologies will solve. Here are those roles (highlighted in Figure 10.2).

What to look for in any infrastructure technology you're considering:

- Make sure that any tech you are contemplating can integrate with your CRM and MAS; otherwise it's pretty much a nonstarter.
- It's also important that the technology integrate with other frequently used systems like Slack and LinkedIn.

Account Selection Technologies
How Do You Get the Right List in Place?

Within the area of account selection, you have the following main categories:

- Data-based tools
- Predictive and intent tools
- Analytics-based tools

In our experience, this is one of the biggest gaps that companies experience when implementing an ABM strategy. In Chapter 4, we discussed not only how critical the target account list is to the success of an ABM effort, but we also talked about how carefully it must be created.

We will go so far as to say that although many businesses have relatively sophisticated infrastructure technologies in place—even if they're not following an ABM strategy—almost no non-ABM companies are sophisticated in the account-selection space.

These technologies help solve the following challenges:

- How to scale the target account list identification process effectively
- How to keep target account lists continuously updated
- How to combine data with qualitative practical knowledge about these accounts

In Figure 10.3, you can see which roles are most affected by account-selection tools, and therefore the people with whom you should discuss the need for additional technology.

What to look for in any account-selection technology you're considering. Can the vendor:

- Identify accounts based on a variety of data, including firmographic, behavioral, and intent signals?
- Go beyond company-level firmographics to understand individual buyers at key accounts?

ROLES AFFECTED:

Marketing Operations	Sales Operations	Demand Generation Manager	Sales/SDRs
Events Manager	Field Marketing	Website Manager	Content Manager
Social Media Manager	Creative/ Designer	In-House Ad Buyer	Sales Enablement

Figure 10.3 Discuss your account-selection tech needs with these people

- Offer fast, self-service implementation?
- Score, rank, and provide insights into existing accounts?
- Help to identify accounts outside of your existing CRM data?
- Offer full transparency into why each company is featured?
- Leverage Artificial Intelligence (AI) technologies to identify buying signals in real time?
- Provide direct activation into marketing channels from the target account list?
- Support the creation of advertising campaigns directly from account lists and filtered account-list audiences?
- Use segmentation defined in the account-selection environment to drive site customization?
- Enable sales-intelligence alerts based on audiences created in the account-selection environment?

Engagement Technologies

How Do You Get a Relevant Message to Your Target Accounts?

In terms of the sheer number of marketing technologies available, this comprises the largest category. They can be grouped into the following main categories:

- Advertising
- Social media
- Website
- Content
- Personalization
- Email
- Events
- Orchestration

Again, almost all businesses have a tech stack that includes items in the preceding list, and even multiple platforms within just one area like social media. With so many tools, it's common to get pushback along the lines of "We don't need yet another content-related tool because we already have several." In our opinion, the better way to think about these technologies is to ask: "Which of these engagement technologies is actually helping us with our ABM-related activities, versus the old approaches that focused on lead volume?" It could be that you're not fully leveraging your existing engagement technologies to support ABM, so that's worth investigating.

ABM-focused engagement technologies help to solve the following challenges:

- Having trouble reaching your target accounts with precision
- Not being able to deliver a targeted message to your most-valuable segments
- Wasting money bringing in accounts that won't buy from you
- Inability to manage programs across channels

When you do a review of these technologies, expect to have multiple meetings with a relatively large group of stakeholders (see Figure 10.4).

What to look for in any engagement technology you're considering. Can the vendor:

- Run campaigns that target key accounts and buying committees within those accounts?
- Protect brand safety through mechanisms like white lists?

ROLES AFFECTED:

Marketing Operations	Sales Operations	Demand Generation Manager	Sales/SDRs
Events Manager	Field Marketing	Website Manager	Content Manager
Social Media Manager	Creative/ Designer	In-House Ad Buyer	Sales Enablement

Figure 10.4   Many stakeholders need to provide input on engagement technologies

- Offer transparency with its white list?
- Provide campaign delivery reporting at the domain level?
- Provide transparency into its targeting data, its sources, and how the data is derived?
- Allow you to serve personalized ads on an anonymous basis?
- Offer dynamic ad creative that is responsive to company, industry, and other attributes at the impression level?
- Allow you to target and personalize advertising using a combination of IP, cookie, and first-party data?
- Provide campaign reporting using B2B metrics?
- Measure the incremental effect of advertising by collecting baseline data or using a control group?
- Identify anonymous visitors?
- Leverage AI technologies to recommend personalized content for every website visitor?
- Let you build customizable, personalized experiences for known and unknown visitors?
- Support integrations with related technologies like CMS and A/B testing platforms?
- Personalize headlines, website heroes, CTAs, and promos, all on a single page?
- Manage your programs, account segments, and messages across all channels?

Of course, ABM can be successful without having all of these capabilities, but they constitute the most complete set of capabilities.

Sales-Enablement Technologies

Marketing Has Done Their Job. How Do You Make Sure Sales Gets It over the Finish Line?

This is the important link between Marketing and Sales, where Marketing has opened the sale through targeting, personalization, and engagement. Now it must provide all the information and collateral for Sales to close the sale.

Sales-enablement tools can be grouped as follows:

- Sales intelligence
- Account insights
- Contact development

These technologies become useful when you're finding a lot of leads going untouched, or not being converted into opportunities. Given that Marketing and Sales have agreed on the target account list, the lack of follow-up should not be due to a mismatch on target account focus. The likely issue is what we discussed in Chapter 9 about the lack of tight coordination on the details of campaigns.

These technologies will help with alerting Sales to the fact that target accounts are visiting certain pages, or downloading materials. They will provide Sales with real-time buying signals from the accounts you collectively care about the most.

People who perform the following roles will want to be around the table when sales-enablement technology is being evaluated (see Figure 10.5).

What to look for in any sales-enablement technology you're considering. Can the vendor:

- Deliver the insights in multiple ways to the sales team? Can it route the information?
- Feed the data into your CRM solution?

ROLES AFFECTED:

Marketing Operations	Sales Operations	Demand Generation Manager	Sales/SDRs
Events Manager	Field Marketing	Website Manager	Content Manager
Social Media Manager	Creative/ Designer	In-House Ad Buyer	Sales Enablement

Figure 10.5   Sales–enablement technology is especially important to people in these roles

- Tell you how the data is collected, and how often the data sources are refreshed?
- Leverage the power of AI to achieve volume and insights far exceeding those through manual methods?

This is a case in which big strides in sales enablement can occur without a big investment: an intranet can often do the job along the lines of the Marketing Center we described in Chapter 9. It's not so much the technology that solves this issue, as it is an obsessive focus on giving Sales the complete content *and context for every campaign.*

Measurement Technologies

How Do You Know What's Working? What's Not? What to Do Next?

It goes without saying that every business measures many things. But an ABM strategy takes measurement to an altogether greater level of granularity.

The kind of technologies that will support ABM fall into these groups:

- Analytics
- Testing and optimization

- Business intelligence
- Attribution and reporting

Here again, it's safe to say that everyone has some of these capabilities. The question is whether your existing tech stack can answer the following questions:

- How can I determine the effect of each of my campaigns?
- What will enable me to share insights with Sales, not just about leads, but about accounts?
- Which messages resonate most with our target accounts?

Although one can make the argument that everyone involved in an ABM effort needs to have the insights that measurement provides, it's going to be the following people who should evaluate technologies (see Figure 10.6).

What to look for in any engagement technology you're considering. Can the vendor:

- Centralize your existing data sources in one location?
- Track B2B metrics by account?
- Offer a dashboard to measure ABM impact from across the funnel?

ROLES AFFECTED:

Marketing Operations	Sales Operations	Demand Generation Manager	Sales/SDRs
Events Manager	Field Marketing	Website Manager	Content Manager
Social Media Manager	Creative/ Designer	In-House Ad Buyer	Sales Enablement

Figure 10.6   Make sure people with these roles are part of the discussion about measurement technologies

- Enable you to create new audiences based on firmographic and intent data to execute across the funnel?
- Track and report on anonymous first-touch visitors by account?
- Allow you to combine first-party and firmographic data for segmentation and reporting?
- Have strategic services in place to help you set up ROI reporting based on your strategy?
- Allow you to compare the performance of different audiences or account lists, evaluate the effect of specific programs, and compare the performance of different vendors?

Now That's a Lot of Reading

For a sales rep to understand the marketing powerhouse, Merkle, at the level that technology and AI allow today, he or she would need to read and interpret two million Google results about Merkle, read around 100,000 pages on merkleinc.com, and then interpret the 68,000 pages of content that Merkel employees produce every month. Next, the rep would have to figure out how all this information relates to his or her company and products. Now multiply that daunting task by hundreds or thousands of accounts, and you have an idea of the power behind AI-driven marketing and sales solutions.

Four Considerations to Keep in Mind

When you're evaluating all these technologies, it's important not just to think about adding technologies, but instead about eliminating other ones. This type of rigorous review of your tech stack may identify cases in which a certain solution worked well two or three years ago, but has since been eclipsed by other solutions. That may be an opportunity for money to be freed up for the more robust solution.

Where possible, look for solutions that can check multiple boxes for you in the following areas:

Data. Make sure the technology can provide comprehensive and insightful data, and that it has the ability to interface with the other technologies you already own. The last thing you need is another "data island" that makes the big picture harder to see.

Scalability. Does the technology allow you to log in to one platform instead of having to log in to multiple places? It might seem like a small matter of just seconds, but you're building an ABM tech stack that can support growth and agility, and you don't need these extra speed bumps if they can possibly be avoided.

Execution. You should look for solutions that help you propagate the same messaging across all your programs and channels.

Cost. Although it can sometimes be less expensive to get a "point solution" that performs one narrow function, be sure to consider the expense of integrating and managing these solutions effectively. Make sure you therefore evaluate the pros and cons of software in the context of overall cost.

We are not suggesting that these become deal-killer criteria in the sense that they must be present or you should reject a solution. You may come across cases in which the solution is so extremely good at what it does that it's worth trying even though it may require a separate log-in or whatever. Your judgment will be the best guide, but it's still useful to keep the preceding criteria in mind.

Take It Step by Step

We think you'll agree that even though we attempted to create some order around 6,800 technology offerings, it's still a daunting task to consider them all.

Just as we recommended that you pilot ABM before scaling, we have a similar recommendation for enhancing your technology: crawl, walk, then run. You were able to develop and run a pilot program with the stack you currently have. You now may have identified a number of pain points in that experience. The best approach is to prioritize which technologies you want to add to your stack, and then implement them in phases.

For each phase, you may be bringing on some new technology, but as we said, you also might be able to eliminate others, along with their associated costs. During a phase, you can determine how it's working for you, and whether it is likely to earn a spot in your stack for the longer term. Also during each phase, you should get enough data for you to calculate an ROI on that new investment. All of this will make it easier to move to the next phase and take maximum advantage of it as well.

In Chapter 4 when we discussed how to create your target account list, we suggested that you designate someone to be the owner of that list: not the most senior person in the room, but instead the go-to person for all list matters. We recommend that you designate an owner of your tech stack for the same reason.

It may be natural to think: "That's what we have an IT department for," but the best owner may not come from IT. When computers were new in organizations a few decades ago, it might have been common for someone in IT to own most aspects of a stack, but things have changed: technology has become so sophisticated that organizations typically have owners of different aspects of technology. For example, there may be different point persons for hardware, the cloud, cybersecurity, and so forth.

It's in that way that we recommend that someone be the owner of the stack as it relates to ABM. It could even be a shared responsibility of a small group. The owner will work closely with Marketing Ops, IT, Sales, and Marketing on ABM-related issues, and will continuously be on top of what's happening in that regard.

We're not necessarily suggesting a new hire, but that during the scale-up and beyond, you have a person or team with a specific KPI that relates to owning the ABM stack. If it's a team, then the KPIs must be specific enough that you don't hear: "I thought he was doing it; ... no; I thought she was doing it ..."

~ ~ ~

With a robust tech stack in hand—or soon to be—what else do you need to know to grow and prosper with ABM? That's the topic of Chapter 11.

11 | Guiding ABM Ever Higher

How to Squeeze the Very Most Benefit from Your ABM Strategy

Wouldn't you say that we've come a long way? You've done the hard work to initiate organizational change such that you could get a pilot off the ground and bring it to a successful conclusion. Then we've discussed the process of proving the ROI of ABM, and how to scale it to other areas of your business.

We've also talked about how to evaluate the technology around an ABM strategy, and how to add capabilities to your tech stack in a methodical way that is supported by ROI data.

In a sense, you now have all you need to grow ABM as large as you'd like it to be in your organization. Actually, we take that back. There's one thing you are missing, and you maybe want to continue to miss—some battle scars.

We like the quote of German Chancellor Otto Von Bismarck, who said: "Fools say that experience is the best teacher. I prefer to learn from other people's experience." That made sense in the nine-teenth century when he was around, and it makes just as much sense in the twenty-first century.

Therefore this next section takes a look at some of the issues that can arise in your own organization as you implement ABM.

The Top Eight Signs that Your ABM Strategy Might Be in Trouble

If you've reached something of a cruising altitude with your ABM strategy, it's certainly cause for feeling gratified. Implementing ABM effectively and growing it is no small accomplishment. After all that hard work, it's time perhaps to ease up on the throttle, but it's also time to stay vigilant about your ABM effort. It's a sophisticated system with countless moving parts, and things can go wrong.

The best way to guard against this happening is to recognize some warning signs. The sooner you identify them, the sooner you can evaluate whether they in fact represent a brewing issue. You'll then be able to take any necessary steps early on, when it's easiest to make course adjustments. Here are the eight most common signs, and what to do about them:

1. Sales leadership stops coming to your meetings

Given the investment your company has made in its ABM strategy, it should be a high priority for leadership from Sales to be engaged in regularly scheduled conversations to assess performance. If your Sales leaders were initially involved but have taken a step back, ask yourself why. Better yet, ask them why. Are they less invested? Less interested? Have they detected an issue that's not been addressed?

Be careful how you ask it, though: when you ask someone "Why aren't you coming to the meetings," you're going to get an answer that supports not coming to the meetings. If you instead ask, "What could we do to make it so you're able to attend more of the meet-ings," then you put the other person on the track of finding solutions, rather than listing objections.

The key is to get them participating again. Maybe that will involve one-on-one conversations, changes to when or where the meetings are held, or something else, but it's crucial that you get to the bottom of the issue, even if it just ends up being meeting fatigue. People notice when leadership shows up or does not show, so open that communication channel. It would not hurt to provide additional success stories and data that continue to validate the ABM approach.

2. Sales keeps changing the target account list

Oh, Sales. We love you. We really do. But it's hard to hit a moving target. You can't keep changing your lineup on us. Set your target account list for a quarter and give us a chance to flex our ABM muscles without rotating players in and out. Down the road, we can see the need to occasionally add someone new here and there, or even get together and reconfigure the entire list after a few sales cycles—but just for one cycle, let's stay consistent with our agreed-upon target account list and let Marketing work its magic.

3. Sales isn't supporting or participating in your programs

When was the last time you asked Sales if a marketing campaign helped them? Or have you asked Sales to name a campaign you ran last quarter? As marketers, we think we work hard to produce effective messaging around creative offers, but none of that matters without the buy-in of the sales team. We all learned way back in ABM 101 that the objectives of Marketing and of Sales need to be aligned. Therefore if you see this lack of support, it's time to talk to some of your buddies in Sales to see what's up, what's changed, and what can be done about it.

4. Someone is still focused on quantity-based metrics

Quantity-based metrics are practically in our DNA. In the ABM world, it's instead about the metrics that matter. You don't hear runners talking about how many steps they ran. Instead, they talk about sport-specific measurements like miles per hour, heart rate, whether they had a PB (personal best) finish, or won the race. These are metrics that move the needle to improve performance. ABM is the same way: it's quality over quantity. It's about hitting the equivalent of that best 10K pace, and it requires agreement from both Sales and Marketing to succeed. Leave those measurements of "connects" and "hand raises" at the starting line, and run with "pipeline," "account engagement," and "revenue."

5. You don't have a healthy (or increasing) number of target accounts on your website

As we know, more than half of the buying process happens on your website. Although you may have an amazing site, if your marketing programs aren't driving your target accounts there, then something is seriously not working according to plan. Check your messaging, your outreach, and your targeting strategy and then make adjustments. Use the ecosystem of your channels, list segmentation, and messaging to attract those targeted accounts to your website.

6. A large percentage of leads are coming from outside your target account list

Repeat (in your head) after us: "Everyone in Marketing needs to focus on the target account list. I will focus on the target account list. I will then segment the target account list by size, by contacts, by steps in the buying process, and by any other ways I can think of, in order to dial in my marketing efforts. I am one with my target account list." Successful ABM requires a laser-like focus on knowing—and marketing to—your targets.

7. The percent of revenue coming from your target account list is dropping quarterly

Although you can always expect some ebbs and flows, most B2B companies typically see 70 to 80 percent of revenue coming from their target account list. If you see it dropping significantly below that, step back and reassess. There may be an issue with your list, or perhaps your sales team has disengaged—you have the warning sign, and now it's time to figure out the root cause. If your numbers drop for one quarter, keep an eye on things, yellow-alert style. If they drop for multiple quarters, that's looking more like red-alert: take action! You won't know what's going on unless you analyze and ask. Your first stop should be over in Sales to begin to figure out what's going on.

8. You can't prove the ROI on your ABM-specific technology

Did you buy specific ABM technology in advance of a full ABM strategy? You did? Well now you can see why it made your job harder down the road, if some of your ROI measurements are weird because you didn't have the proper baseline, or did not measure conversions with and without the technology. The worst case is you thought that purchase would do ABM *for you*.

Moving forward, make sure that you fully build out your ABM strategy before you add more technology. Then follow the steps we've outlined about getting proper baselines and segments, so you're in a position to compare apples to apples. Run for a sales cycle or two and see what your data looks like then. At that point, you can do the tech-stack assessment we talked about in the last chapter, to see what technology you should trim, keep, or add.

You'll notice that none of these signs is insurmountable. The first step is simply to be aware of them, and not just when you're reading this book for the first time. In whatever process document or quarterly reminder system you create, make a note to give your ABM a little physical exam on a regular basis. Where does it hurt? What's been going well and what's an area of concern? How are the lab results looking? What needs immediate attention, and what do we want to keep an eye on? Do this with your colleagues who form the core of the ABM effort.

Granted, it's not the most fun you can have, but it's cheap insurance to keep your significant ABM effort moving in the right direction and producing wins for you.

Two Interesting Questions

Question 1: "What happens when a company implements ABM and has success with it: Is it then inevitable that all units of the company will eventually follow the ABM model, or might there be permanent holdouts?"

The answer is there could be holdouts, for a couple of reasons. First, some B2B businesses are massive, having grown organically and through acquisitions. It could well be that certain business units have a culture or leadership situation that ABM either doesn't fit, or they won't attempt to find out. Fortunately, there's nothing about ABM that requires a company to be 100 percent onboard with it. It's just that the impressive results that come from applying ABM have a way of persuading holdouts that maybe they'd like some of that action, too.

The other reason why some businesses don't apply ABM from the outset is that it doesn't fit with a certain pricing model. For example, one company we work with uses ABM successfully for its enterprise accounts, but they also have a "freemium" plan for their solution, which is just a few dollars a month. They maintain that plan partly because it does bring in a small stream of revenue, and partly because they know that a few of those small companies may grow into enterprise ones over time. For that freemium segment of their business, they're careful to identify target accounts that are good candidates for an eventual upsell. Then they work to nurture and grow those accounts over time into customers of the regularly priced products and services.

Question 2: "How do you people at Demandbase distinguish your approach to ABM in comparison to other companies that teach how ABM should be implemented?"

First, we don't hold a monopoly on how ABM is taught, and there may be some companies that do a fine job of discussing how ABM can be implemented.

Our approach differs in the following ways: we've seen some ABM practitioners overcomplicate matters with a 200-point plan to achieving ABM. In our opinion, that level of detail might be fitting for a company that's been refining its ABM strategy for five years and now is looking for every possible insight to bring it to the next level. The danger is when companies hope to embark on implementing ABM, see a massively complicated plan, and give up before they start.

ABM can be successfully implemented by following the straightforward steps in this book.

Another approach that we find problematic is when companies advocate the early adoption of tech-heavy ABM. You know by now where we stand on that: first get your strategy down, including measurements, processes, communication, and a pilot. Prove ABM in your organization, and then sure, consider technology. We think the tech-first approach is also a prescription for at best, limited success, because it doesn't address some of the underlying organizational issues that ABM has the potential to solve.

CA Technologies Case Study

CA Technologies is a multinational software powerhouse with several billion dollars of annual revenue and more than 11,000 employees. They create many types of software for use in the cloud, on local mainframes, and in countless types of devices.

CA has offices in more than 40 countries and is about as B2B a company as there is. One of their challenges was to try to streamline the customer experience across many different channels.

Their ABM initiative began as a pilot program within the Field Marketing team. CA had faced a few years of declining sales and this group was closely aligned with the team in Sales. The Field Marketing team had a focus to generate pipeline to support Sales. They had previously used the approach of generating volumes of leads through content syndication and other lead-gen efforts, but they weren't working as well anymore.

The first ABM pilot started with a six-month project focused on 125 target accounts. The level of visibility into accounts and their traffic on the site, plus basic lifts were enough to spark interest within CA to expanding ABM.

CA then formed an enterprise list consisting of 2,000 target accounts that were crucial to growing the overall business. They then built out marketing programs to target those accounts across the business units. This second pilot was a full application of analytics, personalization, and smart forms.

Even though CA had the resources to have been able to apply ABM to a larger group of accounts from the outset, they chose to do the pilot first in order to get processes in place, and the level of communication and alignment necessary to be successful.

After the first few months of home page personalization testing, CA had some good data to share. At the same time, they had implemented forms technology that auto-populated company names to ensure data consistency and accuracy.

The combined effort with personalization and forms helped to generate the following results:

- 59 percent increase in average opportunity value
- 17 percent increase in sales velocity
- 237 percent increase in completed forms
- 21 percent increase in close rate
- 121 percent increase in pipeline opportunities

CA also ran an ABM-based ad program for three months to 600 accounts. Here were the results:

- Average contract value was 78 percent higher for accounts that had been exposed to the advertising
- 56 percent increase in page views by the target accounts
- 48 net new target accounts visited the site

There were two other benefits to CA of this ABM effort. The CEO earlier had issued a directive to "create a better customer experience" as one of the key focus areas of the business. Not only had Marketing and Sales delivered the quantitative results mentioned here, but they delivered qualitative benefits in line with that directive through personalized advertising, a multitouch approach, and website personalization.

The second benefit was described as follows by the Global Account-Based Marketing Director at CA:

ABM has helped us provide collaborations across our different teams. We have a huge marketing organization where we've worked in silos. Because of the personalization on CA.com and the analytics, we've had to work very closely with Corporate

Marketing. It's also allowed us to partner with Sales, because we're providing quality data, and we're able to target their top accounts with personalization marketing. We have improved our customer experience across all marketing channels.

What's on the Horizon for ABM

Next Best Action Will Become a Reality

ABM technologies are part of a robust industry that's advancing rapidly. One of the most interesting and potentially rewarding areas to be fully developed over the next few years has to do with what's known as the "next best action."

Let's say a target account attends your webinar. How should you follow up? You could send an email, deliver a white paper, or have an SDR call him or her. You could invite the person to an event, or perhaps to a demo of your solution, or maybe serve an ad. Those are all fine actions among many others, but which one is best?

That has traditionally been answered by someone saying, "What we usually do is …," or "I've had good luck with …," or even "How about we try …?" The challenge here is twofold. First, we're relying on instincts and a marketer's past experience to determine what the next best action is. Second, in this webinar example, all attendees are different: they come from different companies, and they're at different stages of consideration. Marketing to them with a standardized follow-up will neglect those variations. Therefore, for years it's been the dream of marketers to determine the next best action with a system that would be based on solid data.

But even if you did have solid data, the process of determining and executing on the next best action has had a manual component—and any time you have manual intervention, you can't scale that process. You can do it for 100 customers perhaps, but not for the kind of volume you need in order to make a significant business impact.

Here is what is on the horizon: through advancements in machine learning and artificial intelligence, you'll be able to automate the next best action. AI will digest massive amounts of data to understand what kind of company you're coming from, what type of marketer you are, and what type of content you've consumed—both on our website and off.

Then it will look at what you've done in the past in regard to engaging with ads, webinars, SDR follow-up calls, bottles of wine, and other touches—and exactly how effective those things have been in the past. It will be a system that gets more intelligent over time in its recommendations, and it will not be based on hunches, but on probabilities and data. This will enable you to move people more effectively through the buyer's journey and into pipeline and closed–won revenue.

It will also be able to interface with other systems to deliver the next best action: that will even include interfacing with fulfillment companies to deliver that bottle of wine when appropriate, with the right kind of gift note. It will be an exciting and potentially highly effective and profitable mechanism for companies to adopt.

Platforms Will Merge

Right now, MA systems are the predominant platform among most B2B marketers, but in reality, those systems can do only a fraction of what B2B marketers need to accomplish. As a result, marketers also must use CRMs, among other systems, to accomplish the following four actions:

1. **Identify and understand** your target audience
2. **Execute and manage** activities across all touch points and across the funnel
3. **Enable** your sales team so they can develop more pipeline and close more deals
4. **Measure** everything

One of the limitations of MA systems is that they're designed exclusively for individuals. For example, they are great at loading individual contacts into a database and then emailing them. That's an important function, but only a small part of the overall functionality that's necessary.

When companies embrace the power of ABM, they realize that they need to engage not only with individuals, but also with accounts as a whole. Therefore, you need to be able to accomplish the four actions mentioned here at both the individual and the account level. Today, MA systems do about 1.5 of those four things well: they can identify, execute, and measure, but only at the individual level.

We believe over the next few years a single platform will emerge that will more effectively do the work that these multiple systems do today. This system will substantially automate and streamline what marketers for decades have done through cobbling together various systems.

Maybe this single platform will be dominated by a single vendor, or it could be multiple vendors that offer similar, but truly comprehensive, functionality for B2B marketers. Although we don't know how this will unfold, we are confident that this general trend will happen. The Martech landscape is just too confusing and fragmented as it stands now—too many companies are struggling to string together point solutions and connect their data for this to continue.

We trust you've seen throughout this book some of the astonishing potential that ABM has for taking B2B business up a few levels. When you consider these technologies on the horizon, well, it's going to be one exciting ride.

~ ~ ~

We've reached the end of this book, but the good news is it's only the end of the beginning!

Our goal has been to give you a tour through the powerful strategy that is Account-Based Marketing. If you've stayed with us through all the details of how to set up your pilot, scale up afterward, and keep it all on track, then we're impressed. From where we sit, as practitioners of ABM, we think that your finishing this book is a pretty good signal that you are serious about trying this strategy in your company.

As surprising as it may sound, coming from a company that provides ABM solutions worldwide, we're also serious when we say it again: you don't need sophisticated software to get off the ground with ABM.

You have in your hands—and now in your head—the principles of focusing on accounts and revenue; the alignment between Sales and Marketing; the reliance on data and measurement to guide your next steps; and the other experience-based insights you read about in this book.

Now is the time for the one thing this or any other book cannot provide: taking action. Fortunately, there are no leaps necessary, just the willingness to take one logical step after another to get that pilot up and running.

Remember what we said way back in Chapter 1: ABM is at its sweet spot of development as far as you should be concerned. It's been used and refined by many B2B businesses around the world. But the technology is new and rapidly changing that enables some of the most sophisticated uses of ABM. It's our hope that you are rewarded for taking action to implement ABM in your organization by being able to capture an outsized portion of the target accounts you care about, before your competitors figure it out. You now know what to do.

Acknowledgments

This book would not have been possible without the amazing contributions of Demandbase employees, past and present, as well as customers, partners, analysts, and other thought leaders. We have been honored to work with some of the smartest people in the industry as we have developed and fine-tuned the strategies and best practices found in this book. Below is a partial list of the individuals who have made significant contributions to the development of Account-Based Marketing and this book.

Phil Hollrah
Mimi Rosenheim
Lisa Ames
Nani Schaffer
John Dering
Lia Hansen
Beth Tiltges
Stephanie Thomas
Christine Farrier
Leanne Chesco
Rory Tokunaga
Matt Aaronson
Rahul Patwardhan
Adam Nichols

Luis Romero
Jonah Phillips
Erica Perng
Tenessa Lochner
Stephen Scowcroft
Jay Tuel
Don White
Gabe Rogol
Mark Yatman
Alan Fletcher
Aman Naimat
Rachel Balik
Matthew Miller
John Arnold
Chris Souza
Kathy Macchi
Rob Leavitt
Bev Burgess
Shari Johnston
Matt Heinz

The talented analysts at Forrester, Gartner, TOPO, and Sirius Decisions

And Jonathan Rozek, who's talented writing, editing, and guidance was instrumental in transforming all of our words and thoughts into this comprehensive guide.

Index

Page numbers followed by *f* refer to figures.